WORD OF MOUTH

WORD OF MOUTH

A Guide to Commercial and Animation Voice-Over Excellence

3rd Edition, Revised and Updated

Susan Blu | Molly Ann Mullin | Cynthia Songé

SILMAN-JAMES PRESS   LOS ANGELES

10 9 8 7 6 5 4 3 2 1

Library of Congress Cataloging-in-Publication Data

Blu, Susan.
Word of mouth : a guide to commercial and animation
voice-over excellence / by Susan Blu, Molly Ann Mullin, and
Cynthia Songé. -- 3rd ed.
p. cm.
ISBN-13: 978-1-879505-87-2
1. Voice-overs. 2. Voice culture--Exercises. I. Mullin, Molly Ann. II.
Songé, Cynthia. III. Title.

PN4197.B56 2006
808.5--dc22

2006022212

Cover design by Wade Lageose

Photographs by Ben Martin © 1986, except where noted otherwise.

Earlier editions of *Word of Mouth* were published by Pomegranate Press, Ltd.

Printed and bound in the United States of America

Silman-James Press
1181 Angelo Drive
Beverly Hills, CA 90210

CONTENTS

FOREWORD

$\mathcal{A}$ s an actress I'm more than impressed with Susan Blu's, Molly Ann Mullin's and Cynthia Songé's "handbook" for people involved in and aspiring to become a part of the very unique voice-over industry.

Cartoon work and industrial as well as commercial copy is dealt with in the same manner that actors approach characters for film, television, and theater. What is their personal history, where are they, what is their goal—in essence for me it is similar to the Stanislavsky method of examining and building a character.

The result is not just a disembodied voice, but contains the texture of one human being really speaking to another. Therefore, the audience can identify and relate to what is being said. For the seasoned voice-over artist as well as the newcomer, this book is invaluable.

It takes us on the journey from the desire to become a part of the voice-over world to the culmination of the first job. Sue, Molly Ann, and Cynthia share their personal and professional experience and wisdom to make *Word of Mouth* a must for everyone in the specialized voice-over industry.

Jessica Walter

PREFACE

MORE OUT OF THE BLU

*T*HANKS TO ALL OF you who have helped make *Word of Mouth* a bestselling guide to voice-over excellence. While the book has gone through many printings and updates over the years, I thought the time was right to produce a completely new edition that would address all the technological changes that have developed in our industry since *Word of Mouth* was first published in 1987. I also felt that this was a good time to check in with all of you and give you some of my thoughts and feelings about our careers in the world of voice-overs—and maybe my thoughts about the world. No; I'll save that last part for another book.

To help us with our revision, Molly Ann Mullin and I asked Cynthia Songé, a voice artist and casting director, to give us a hand. Molly Ann continues to work as a writer and voice artist. I have been spending the last several years performing in voice-overs and directing actors in animation.

I have learned some useful things working in the voice-over field, an occupation nowhere near as unusual as some of you may have thought it to be. There are many more voice-over actors working now, and it's been fun and exciting to experience this growth in the industry. I say, "The more the merrier," and hope that reading *Word of Mouth* encouraged many of you to enter the voice-over business. Yes, there's more competition for all of us, but as a friend once said to me, "The cream rises to the top."

I've also been asked, "Why do you teach classes?" "Why did you write a book?" "Why invite more people into our secure little circle of voice-over artists?"

Molly Ann and I wrote the book because no one else at the time had produced a book on voice-overs. As an experienced voice-over artist and teacher, I felt I was as qualified as anyone to share some expertise, advice, and instruction on the topic. Someone would eventually write a how-to manual on voice-overs, and—hey!—why not be the first? Of course, there are many more books out now on the field of voice-overs. Some I have read, some I haven't. I believe any book is worth examining if you're interested in getting into the field. The more information you can acquire and assimilate, the better you will be at taking and using what works for you.

In looking back through the pages of our book, I believe that, after all the years it has been used for individual and classroom instruction, it still works. The book will never be outdated because it deals with the fundamental elements of achieving excellence in voice-over. Some of the heroes who shared their expertise in this informative little book are no longer with us, but their wisdom and my memories of them will never be forgotten.

Meanwhile, there have been many technological changes in our industry. Much of the equipment recording studios now use is incredibly high-tech—and evolving all the time. State-of-the-art studios use Pro Tools software, synthesizers, and lots of fancy doodads—I'm surprised they haven't tried to replace us! Well, they have tried, but unsuccessfully. Somehow, they can't replace the magic coming from words spoken from a real heart and soul, and individual hearts and souls working together. Voiceprints—like fingertips and snowflakes—are all beautifully unique, spectacular, and special.

I remember on my first demo recording, how each spot had to be spliced together using a razor blade! The process took a very long time. Now editing is done digitally. You can shift everything around and use it or lose it anywhere you want—*voilà*, you have a demo recording in no time at all. But remember, I am just talking about the technical aspects of producing the recording. It still takes a ton of effort, time, and talent to produce a great demo.

Among other changes, reel-to-reel tapes and cassette tapes are no longer used. We now use CDs. Instead of going to an agent's office for an audition, we can now do it through our computers in our homemade studios—sometimes nothing more elaborate than a converted closet—and send it by e-mail to agents or producers anywhere in the world. Voicebank is an Internet server we use to send and listen to auditions. We can go to Voicebank.net, where voiceover agents post their client's demos for the world to hear. It is so much easier (and cheaper!) than having to send our demo to hundreds of advertisers and animation casting directors.

For me, the fact that I can be on a golfing holiday on the Central Coast of California, enjoying the ocean and a beautiful sunset, and still be able to take time out to send an audition by e-mail is a remarkable, wonderful advantage not available when Molly and I wrote the first edition of this book.

I know a talented promo actor who recorded his promos from bed after a serious operation. Many of the promo people that you hear doing their thing—as in, "Stay tuned, coming up next"—have their own home-made recording studios. I have to admit, I like to get out of the house, see people, and have an intelligent, amusing conversation with my V.O. cronies. Also, it reminds my agents what I look like, and I think that sort of contact is important. Besides, dialogue spots between two or more people make up a large portion of our work in commercials, and we can't do that at home by ourselves.

Another thing that I am thrilled to report is that, even though I'm older, my voice is still the same as it was when this book first hit the stores. I can still play kid voices to old, funny character voices with ease. Actually, maybe I'm even a bit better now that I've come to care less about having to get every single job and more about the fun and passion for the work itself that I'm experiencing on a daily basis. Don't misunderstand! I love getting the job, winning the audition. But now I have a heartfelt appreciation that the right jobs are mine and the others are yours. I know that there really is room for all of us. What it takes to join this select group is talent, passion, perseverance, and a belief in oneself that can't be shaken, rocked, or questioned. There is always room for excellent new performers who will risk and take the chances to allow the creativity to come through.

Every one of my gifted students who has stuck with it is successful. I've had people come through my booth to audition for an animated series, actors whom I have never met before who are just terrific and original in their choices for the role, and they get the part. When an actor comes in for an audition prepared with some interesting choices for the character, is fun to work with and easy to direct, but is not quite right for that particular role, I will bring them back again. I always have a large percentage of new people in the shows I direct. When I become your fan and want to champion you, I will do everything I can to find the right role for you.

My priority is to cast people who will make a great ensemble, and who I know will be able to come through for me under pressure. In those

xiv   W O R D   O F   M O U T H

not-so-relaxed sessions with story editors, producers, toy-company executives, animators, and who knows who else, my actors need to deliver a line in the script several different ways until everyone is happy—and do so with a smile. With only four hours to get a show recorded, I want the studio to be upbeat, relaxed, and harmonious.

A word about nerves: Coming into the studio a bit nervous can sometimes be beneficial. A rush of adrenaline, with your nerves tingling with excitement, can lift your talent to the next level of excellence. Embrace your nerves and use that energy to let phenomenal choices come through you.

With all of the new cable channels and other venues that have come into existence since this book was written, the volume of work in voice-over and animation is now huge. Every time I turn on the television, there is a new cartoon series or a new commercial. The talent never ceases to amaze me. Almost every actor wants to do an animation project, and I've had the wonderful chance to direct some fabulously talented celebrities. But even when we use a well-known name, we usually surround that person with veteran voice actors to round out the ensemble. Usually, when we are casting a new voice for a series, we are looking for an unknown who will create the character and become identified with it. But in the series *Clifford, The Big Red Dog*, the late John Ritter—who was well-known, much-loved—was cast in the role of Clifford, bringing a wonderful vulnerability and personality to that loveable dog.

My feeling is that as long as there are children in the world and as long as there is the child in all of us, cartoons will be made. Animated characters range in type from very real-sounding human characters to zany, funny, cartoony objects, like a sponge that can talk. Know how to do it all. By the way, there are not a lot of women who do great kid voices. If you can develop a believable kid-like vocalization, you have a better chance of working in the animation field.

Your ability to create special, unique characters is the secret to success. Create outside the box—ask yourself, "What is it I can do to make this voice, this character, different from the other people auditioning for this job?" When a casting director asks you to do the copy less cartoony, they are telling you to try to make the character more believable, someone we can relate to and identify with. A character—even a sponge—that can make us laugh or make us cry is a believable character. That is a character that we will want to see and hear again and again.

Be true to yourself, and know yourself as well as you can so you can bring an emotion to a character that is unique to you. Put your talent on the line, and take risks by making original choices. Dig deep and find the creativity in you that wants to surface and be revealed. Take chances with your creative decisions, and show yourself through your creativity. You will be special and will stand out in a crowd of talented people if you simply put your true self in your work and find the spark that will ignite the excitement inside of you.

ACKNOWLEDGMENTS

*T*HE AUTHORS WISH TO gratefully acknowledge the many people who contributed so willingly and generously to this book.

Our deep appreciation to: Carlos Alazraqui, June Allyson, Jack Angel, Allison Argo, Paul Armbruster, Edward Asner, Dee Baker, Larry Belling, Stephen Blackwell, Bobbi Block, Devon Bowman, Wayne Brady, Kathi Brandt, Charlotte Ann Bulow, Greg Callahan, Nancy Cartwright, Timothy Casto, Cathy Cavadini, Angela M. Chance, Cam Clarke, Philip L. Clarke, Ellen Cockrill, Sid Conrad, Elaine Craig, Brian Cummings, John B. Curtis, Jeff Danis, Jennifer Darling, Diane Davenport, Donna Lee Davies, Smae Spaulding Davis, Flo Di Re, Brian Donovan, Deborah Forte, Pat Fraley, Nika Futterman, Kelly Garner, Linda Gary, Dick Gautier, Richard Gittelson, Marsha Griffin, Chet Grissom, Jess Harnel, Aldis Hodge, Gordon Hunt, Marcia Hurwitz, Gordon Jump, Tom Kenny, Kathy and Eric King of Photoking Labs, Paul Kirby, Jonathan Kirsch, Chuck Kourouklis, Linda Kwan, Michael Laskin, Kathy Levin, Mary McDonald Lewis, Lucy Liu, Robert T. Lloyd, Sherry Lynn, Wm H. Macy, Natalina Maggio, Roger Marks, Brian McWilliams, Ginny McSwain, David Meyer, Leanne Moreau, Robert Morse, Pat Musick, Nicholas Omana, Audu Paden, Patrick Pinney, Thom Pinto, Pam Predisik, Mike Rad, Robert Ridgley, Marcy Robin, Andrea Romano, Colette Romero, Sandie Schnarr, Michael Sheehan, Jamie Simone, Michael Smith, Kath Soucie, Fred Stoller, James Arnold Taylor, Arlene Thornton, Rita Vennari, Brian Veronica, Lea Vernon, Jessica Walter, B.J. Ward, Isabella Way, Jill Wayne, Beau Weaver, Rick Weis, Libby Westby, John Westmoreland, Betty White, Henry Winkler.

We would also like to thank entertainment attorney Sam Sacks, copyright attorney Paul D. Supnick, and publishers Gwen Feldman and Jim Fox for their contributions and support.

A special thanks to all those who have provided comfort and courage along the way. The include: Hazel M. and John Harrison Blu, J.W. (Bud) Mullin, Marian M. Hancock, Al Martin, Richard Rosen, and many other dear (and tolerant!) friends whom we love very deeply.

INTRODUCTION

*W*HAT IS A VOICE-OVER? A commercial voice-over is the audio portion of a radio or television sales or promotional spot. That is an industry definition, and now that you know it, you can forget it—except for those times when your puzzled friends and relatives want to know why you are making all those strange noises.

Our own definition focuses on you, the artist. We like to say that voice-over is the opportunity for you to look inside yourself, to find and become all the different people you already are. A voice-over is not just someone reading a commercial—it is a particular person, in a particular situation, talking to another particular person (or persons), about a particular product.

Notice we said that you *become* certain people. Voice-over excellence requires acting in the finest sense of the word. Don't panic, all you non-actors out there. All this means is that to deliver believable ad copy, you must get in touch with the reality of the Speaker, as well as the circumstances surrounding him or her. And we'll show you how to do just that. Remember, even if the Speaker you are asked to do is described in the minutest detail—down to freckles, frown, and flat feet—the Speaker you actually become is still just one of those many people you already have inside you. We'll help you find them, too. If you enjoy meeting new people, you'll love the discoveries you're going to make.

Now we'd like you to do a bit of soul-searching. Take a moment and answer this question: Why are you so interested in doing voice-overs? To make piles of money? To do something different? People have said that you have an interesting voice, but you don't know what to do with it? You're a ham, but there's not enough pork in you to go in front of the camera? Any reason is valid, but just know what your choice is so you can focus on it for motivation during the tough times.

Our purpose is to give you the information you need to function as an excellent voice-over artist. Although this book is basically an introduction to the world of voice-overs, the techniques and methods we discuss work just as well for the seasoned professional as for the beginner.

How can a career in voice-overs begin? Molly Ann enrolled in Susan's voice-over classes just for fun. "I wanted to play with the spoken rather than the written word for a change, and you couldn't get me up on a stage or in front of a camera if you took my whole family hostage." With that first class, Molly Ann was hooked.

Cynthia Songé worked as an actor for years. After taking classes from Susan Blu, she began a successful voice-over career. She teaches Susan Blu's voice-over technique, produces and directs voice-over demos, and assists Susan in many of her casting projects.

Susan Blu had an active career as an actress, singer, and cabaret performer when she got a call from her agent. "If you were the Pillsbury Dough Girl, what would you sound like?" At that point, Susan didn't even know what a voice-over was. She thought a moment, envisioned the role, and "a voice just came out." She was selected to be the official Pillsbury Dough Girl with a lucrative two-year contract. Susan freely credits her ignorance for a large portion of her early voice-over success. "I didn't know it could be difficult, so I never thought I couldn't do it. As I became more experienced, I started hearing the stories about how tough it could be. Rather than believe them, I started to study and get into classes to learn voice-over techniques, which I still practice every day."

Susan has done literally thousands of commercial and animation voice-overs. She has been heard in roles such as: Granny Smurg in *The Smurfs*, Flim Flam in *Scooby-Doo*, *The Flintstone Kids*, Arcee in *The Transformers*, and many more. Susan is a renowned voice director in animated series as well as in feature films. Many of these shows have been nominated for the coveted Emmy award. Some of the shows that she voice-directed include: *The Land Before Time* videos and DVDs, *Clifford the Big Red Dog* feature film and television series, *Stuart Little III*, the feature and the animated series, *Spider-Man*, *Jackie Chan Adventures*, *The Magic School Bus*, *American Tale*, and numerous others. Susan began her directing career with *Teenage Mutant Ninja Turtles*. When her schedule permits, she still teaches an animation voice-over class in Los Angeles.

With practice you, too, can acquire a positive, professional attitude and develop the excellent skills that will lead to a successful and rewarding career in voice-overs. And, while we are delighted that you are reading and using this book, and listening to the CD we've produced to accompany it, we heartily encourage you to get to the point where you can finally put these tools down and go forth to do voice-overs. This book and CD will always be available for reference, but you must develop your own skills and instincts and trust your own feelings about this business.

Our approach is a very positive one. We believe that the time and energy people spend dwelling on the negatives (I can't; I'm afraid; I'll never get this; etc.) are wasted. If people were to spend the same time and energy on the positives, they would soon achieve excellence in the field of voice-over work.

We like to keep the entire learning process a game and not think of it as a goal. Goals tend to focus on the result, and they leave little or no room for the process, which is where the real fun and creativity take place. Games keep you in the process and out of the result. We will be making this point again and again because we firmly believe that if you concentrate on and stay in the process, the desired results will automatically come.

If you aren't having fun doing voice-overs, do yourself a favor and get out of the business. The least bit of boredom or unhappiness will show up in your voice and everyone will be aware of it. A camera does not lie, and neither does a microphone.

Winning the game is important. Getting an agent or getting that job really does matter. But winning traditionally signals the end of the game. According to voice-over actor Jack Angel, in voice-overs you win by simply choosing to play the game. So treat each step you take to acquire and maintain voice-over excellence as a game—a fun place to visit—then move on to the next step and enjoy it, too. And now . . . let the games begin!

1.

HOW TO BEGIN

HEN APPROACHING ANYTHING NEW, we often bring with us certain misconceptions. Let's begin by destroying five popular myths about the voice-over business.

1. VOICE-OVERS ARE MALE-DOMINATED.

If you were to keep track of how many commercials are done by men compared to women, you would indeed find that the majority of spots are done by men. However, in the past decade, females of all ages have taken a solid place in every aspect of the voice-over industry: commercial, animation, promos, and trailers. Ad agencies are much less tied to the old concept that women can buy anything but they can't sell it. Agency executives are now far more supportive of women artists in the voice-over field and are actively looking for fresh new female talent. Ladies and gentleman, the arena is open and there is room for everyone.

2. THERE IS A CLIQUE IN THE INDUSTRY.

This implies that the same people work all the time and there's no room for newcomers. While those of us with established careers are grateful to be rewarded for our skill and experience by being re-hired, the doors of opportunity for new arrivals are wide open. Let us re-emphasize that the search is definitely on for new voice-over artists. And while the field is undoubtedly opening up to women, it is also in need of fresh new male talent.

Again, so much has changed in the past decade, largely because of technology and the advent of the Internet. In the past, casting directors held auditions in offices and studios where only a limited number of actors could be recorded in a day. Now agents and casting directors are utilizing such systems as Voicebank.net, an online service that we will discuss in more detail later. Instead of hearing perhaps 100 auditions per session, casting directors can listen to several hundred actors. Yes, that means competition is even more fierce, but it also means that there is greater opportunity for everyone.

Andrea Romano, animation casting and voice director, says: "There is always room in this business for anyone who has excellent animation and commercial talent."

Excellent talent—that's the key. Because the bar, or standard of excellence, has been raised to new heights. Today, in order to enter the voice-over field, it is necessary to have great skill and talent. That is the real clique . . . not restricted to already well-established voice-over talent, but open to anyone possessing voice-over excellence.

Animation casting and voice director Ginny McSwain draws on her background in casting, directing, and agenting to add a word of caution: "Without being negative—just realistic—you must be aware of how many people want to do voice-overs for a living, and how many artists are already paying their mortgages from voice-overs alone. You must have a healthy insight into competition.

"Being in touch with your own voice, constantly practicing and training to hone your skills—plus having the strong desire to put your own vocal signature on the air—can keep you in prime shape to win those jobs."

3. YOU NEED TO HAVE AN UNUSUAL VOICE.

If you were blessed with the power of speech, you already have something about your natural voice that makes it different or special. In fact, your voice is unique; no one else has one identical to yours.

Given a large enough sample of phonemes (the sounds we use to make words), experts can use the vocal equivalent of fingerprints, called voiceprints, to positively identify one speaker from all others. One of your first steps will be to find out what the "special something" in your voice is . . . it is often found close to your heart.

People do get into this business because their voices "sound so different." They have an unusual accent or rhythm or pitch—and that gets them work, but many of these people do not last. Why? Because they don't bother to study and develop voice-over excellence.

They have hit on one way of delivering copy, and they use it over and over again. When directed to change in the delivery, they are at a loss. Once the novelty wears off, they are no longer in demand; those who can take direction and have developed vocal flexibility are the ones who have long-term voice-over careers. If your voice has a particular signature, great . . . embrace your strengths, and learn how to fully exploit your gift.

However, for those of us who do not have a certain signature in our voice, the benefit is that we will be less identifiable as the spokesperson for one specific product. Producers won't tire of hearing us.

A producer of many commercial spots, Nicholas Omana says: "Flexibility is very important. Over the years, I've seen different vocal styles come and go. Yesterday it was the more aggressive hard-sell. Today they want a softer, more laid-back approach. You must be able to change in order to keep working."

Using voice-over artist Thom Pinto as an example, Nicholas adds: "You know, even Thom says he doesn't have a great or unusual voice. He has an anonymous voice, but that man works all the time! He has the ability to meld his voice into many different characters. Producers never get tired of hearing him because he's always someone different. Even his close friends don't always recognize him in the spots he's done. The more versatile and chameleon-like you are, the more you will work."

THOM PINTO

Elaine Craig of Elaine Craig Voicecasting says, "Voice-over actors should have the flexibility to change their preconceived ideas of how the copy should be read when I give them various directions. For instance, I have directed actors who insist on reading the copy according to their own interpretation, closing their minds to my direction—and therefore limiting their chances of landing the job. The ability to listen and interpret the given direction is often more important to me than the quality of their voices."

4. YOU HAVE TO BE A CERTAIN AGE TO DO CERTAIN CHARACTERS.

What age? Which characters? We believe that voice-over excellence does not involve "doing a sixty-year-old voice," for example. Rather, it involves becoming a particular sixty-year-old character.

The appropriate voice will come automatically.

Voice-overs are delightfully ageless. Each voice has built-in physical characteristics that allow the artist to make certain age and sex crossovers. Susan has done a number of young-boy characters because of the lower pitch and natural crack in her voice. "Women have more opportunities here," she says. "Once a boy's voice has changed, chances are he can no longer produce a believable pre-adolescent male voice."

Producers prefer to cast adults to play children's parts, but they don't always think of a woman playing the part of a male youth. On one occasion there was a casting call for the role of a young boy. Susan's agent succeeded in persuading the producers to give Susan an audition. The agent's persistence paid off—Susan got the role. We encourage you to keep practicing and stretching to do characters of both sexes and, barring any physical limitations to your vocal range, you can create believable male and female characters of many different ages.

5. YOU MUST ALREADY BE A PROFESSIONAL ACTOR.

Cunningham, Escott, Slevin, Dipene and Associates Vice President Dona Lee Davies (whose background includes casting, production, and agenting) says: "This is absolutely not true. Anyone who develops voice-over excellence can make it in this business. However, in order to develop voice-over excellence and to read well, you must learn to act." Those of you who wouldn't take an acting class at gunpoint are probably mentally packing your bags right now and taking the next plane out of here. Don't go! Hear us out. You can always catch a later flight.

Eventually you may decide to do a few acting workshops. A good voice-over class should include acting technique: learning how to express attitudes, personality, and emotions authentically. Although studying other areas of our craft such as acting classes, improvisation, singing and dance are not a requirement, they can only benefit in developing the actor's instrument.

Acting involves getting in touch with the reality of a particular person in a particular situation. What makes it real is you—reaching inside YOURSELF to draw on your own experience to become that person in that situation. And that's what voice-overs are all about.

Somewhere inside, you have stored everyone and everything you have ever experienced. In this business we are privileged to enter that treasure room and sample and explore to our heart's delight. Inside, we discover various aspects of our own personality and emotions as well as a multitude of different people who have been there all along, just waiting for us to find them.

So much for the myths. We hope you can lay them to rest, for believing them will only give them the power to exist. And, existing, they will leave no room in your world for voice-over success. Now that you are open to success, let's look at what it takes to launch your voice-over career. First, there are the physical essentials:

A VOICE.

Just having one is not enough. What you choose to do with that voice is what really counts.

AN AUDIO RECORDER.

You will work extensively with this machine, which will give you feedback on your progress. Only by hearing your readings, or "takes," can you learn to analyze and critique your own performance.

AD COPY.

This is the material you will be learning to interpret—not just to read—in order to get in touch with its reality. (See the Exercises at the end of this chapter.)

A PENCIL.

In Chapter Three, you will find a system (or you may create your own) of marking copy to help you remember specific emotions or put emphasis on certain words or phrases.

A STOPWATCH.

Also in Chapter Three, you will learn how to work with a stopwatch to develop an exact sense of timing.

A CLASS.

Why bother with a class when you can read a voice-over workbook and learn all the basics? Because a class is the place where you can take risks or "stretch," and get immediate, expert feedback from a professional. It is where you can learn and practice your craft in front of a microphone in a professional booth. Students should continue to study, and learn from various teachers or coaches. As Susan says, "Those who work a lot, work a lot, because they work a lot."

An audition is not the place to try something new. But in a good voice-over class, the environment is supportive. You will be encouraged to explore and develop all dimensions of your voice and learn your strengths and weaknesses. There are other, less tangible, essentials that we feel are equally important.

1. An imagination.

You must be able to visualize yourself as—in order to become—a specific person in a specific situation.

2. A willingness to take/make time to work.

Attending class once a week or skimming through a workbook without ever doing your homework will get you nowhere fast. As with anything that we truly desire, we must have a willingness matched with a commitment to do the work and take the necessary steps. One does not join a gym, work out for six weeks with a personal trainer, and expect to keep that level of fitness without continuing to train, to work out. Our voice is a muscle, and we are finely tuned instruments that require constant attention and maintenance.

The pursuit of voice-over excellence requires that you do certain exercises and practice recommended techniques as often as possible—then make time to do them some more.

3. A willingness to play.

While you are learning and growing, be mindful not to judge yourself. Critique is useful. Judging can be harmful and stifle our willingness to take chances.

Becoming all sorts of different people is exciting if you approach it with the joyful abandon with which children play. Even the most shy child grows bold when he or she "becomes" another person. Remember, it's your game you are playing, so don't waste time being shy with yourself—and no stinking thinking!

QUESTIONS:

What sort of audio recorder do I need?

One that is easy and comfortable for you to work, that gives you clear playbacks, and that you can reasonably afford. Some students prefer to work with more sophisticated technology, using computer programs that are designed for recording. More of this easy and affordable technology continues to be developed. If you go this route, you will also require a decent microphone (and mic stand). You also might consider buying a music stand so that you will be accustomed to reading as you would in a professional recording booth.

Can I make it in the business?

Yes . . . but making it is a relative term. As with most careers in the arts, we are never guaranteed income or employment from one job to the next. With talent, willingness, confidence, and determination, you can throw your hat in the ring with other talented artists . . . then keep working at your craft and enjoy the journey.

Voice-over actors are unique, and different from other actors in that they can be cast in a range of roles that have nothing to do with gender, age, or appearance. They have limitless opportunities to stretch and grow. In one day, they may go on several auditions or jobs, and be called upon to come up with a number of different characters. While the on-camera or stage actor works with only one director, the voice-over artist may work with several different directors all in the same day.

This takes a special kind of person—flexible, professional, willing to take risks, and committed to excellence.

What are the various types or categories of voice-over spots?

Voice-overs are usually either commercial or animation. Both categories include single (one-person spots), doubles (two-person spots), and multiples (spots which call for more than two people).

Commercial: voice-overs for products or services as ads on radio and television. These are often scripted as a scene with an announcer (or spokesperson) and two or more voice-over actors as commercial characters. More often than not, the client is looking for "real" sounding voices with conversational reads. Listeners then have the feeling that someone is actually talking to them.

Animation: characters for cartoons. There is a variety of genres: cartoons, action-adventure, and feature. This is where the voice actor can show acting and vocal range by the characters they create.

Promos and trailers: the voice announcing upcoming programming on television or enticing us to theaters to see feature film releases.

Industrials: informative short films, educational or corporate. Often actors will be called upon to read ten to twenty pages of technical terminology. They must learn the correct pronunciation and be prepared to record the piece in a single take.

Books on tape: audio recordings of books intended for purposes of either education or pleasure.

What is the difference between commercial and animation work?

According to Susan, "Because both involve acting, commercial and animation voice-overs have the same starting point—a slice of life. But whereas commercial voice-overs typically call for a heightened sense of reality, animation voice-overs require an exaggeration of life."

Animation work (supplying voices for cartoon characters or inanimate objects) is extremely colorful, and calls for very versatile actors with many different, often far-out, character voices. There is absolutely no room for inhibitions in animation work. Its sole purpose is to entertain.

Entertainment is a secondary concern to commercial voice-overs; they must leave the listener remembering the name of the product. Also, commercials are not as vivid as animation voice-overs; they call for layers of subtlety on a base of sincerity.

Susan Blu

Do voice-over artists specialize in any one area?

Many voice-over actors specialize in only one category, while some are versatile enough to work in all areas. Each category requires special skills and abilities.

Some voice-over artists prefer animation; others love commercials. It's a matter of personal preference. The animation talent enjoys the hyper, off-the-wall animation work and is bored silly by commercials. The commercial talent prefers the more subtle, toned-down approach of commercials.

Do some voice-over artists specialize in promos?

Sure. Some voices are more suited to being straight announcers. These artists have discovered a strength and are capitalizing on it. This field of voice-over work is especially lucrative because, by their nature, promos must be constantly changed and updated.

What about industrials?

We'll let John Westmoreland, with his extensive background in producing voice-over spots, answer this one.

"Voice-over artists do specialize in the area of industrials or informational films, and I have tremendous respect for these people. They are responsible for doing ten to twenty pages of copy filled with technical terms that would make your hair curl. When they are given the copy ahead of time, they look up every single word and come in for a session completely prepared and able to offer alternative pronunciations. They also don't get the multiple takes that regular commercial spots are allowed because there just isn't time—but these people are always economical with our time. Doing voice-overs for the military is even worse, because your access to the copy is often restricted. Talent must go where the copy is being recorded or where it was written, read it there, and then record it right away."

I've done some work as a DJ. Will this help me get into voice-overs?

NICHOLAS OMANA

Former DJ Nicholas Omana says: "I learned a lot about the technical aspects of working in a studio while I was a DJ, but that alone did not prepare me to make the transition. DJs don't always have the acting ability required to do voice-overs and, frankly, I found the work boring.

"When you are a DJ, you're the same person all the time; with voice-overs, you can be a lot of different people. Doing voice-overs, I have a basic metabolic rate that is twenty percent higher than in any of my other jobs. Voice-over work is more immediate and it calls for a quick study. Plus, there are a variety of ways to go within your own vocal and attitudinal range."

I've had acting classes. Isn't that enough?

No! While acting classes are certainly desirable, there are many techniques and skills that are unique to voice-overs. It is a different medium. Susan says: "As our eyes don't lie on film, our voices don't lie in voice-over. Ultimately it is the art of reading, giving the illusion that we are not reading while we lace it with our heart and soul. Unlike on-camera acting, where we take our eyes off of the page to make eye-contact, in voice-over we must keep our eyes on the page in order to take the words off of the page."

If there are so many voice-over classes around, how do I find out about them and how do I pick the right one for me?

Voice-over classes are advertised in the trade papers, such as *Backstage West, Daily Variety,* and the *Hollywood Reporter.* Be sure to check our Resources chapter at the back of this book, and check out the Internet for listings. Before enrolling in a class, investigate the instructor's credentials and ask the following important questions:

- How large are the classes?
- How much mic time are students given?
- Are there guest speakers (agents, casting directors, other working voice-over professionals, etc.)?
- How much do the classes cost?

Reputation is extremely important, so ask around for recommendations. Then, if possible, arrange an interview with the teacher or request permission to audit a class to see if the methods, approach, and attitude of the instructor fit your needs.

Samantha Paris—voice actor, casting director, and teacher—opened Voicetrax in Sausalito, California, to provide a training center that is completely professional, but also fun and creative—a place where people could feel comfortable exploring their talent and "feel safe even when they fall flat on their faces." She says, "Success in voice-over isn't some God-given talent that some people have and others don't. In my heart,

SAMANTHA PARIS

I believe that anyone with a desire to do voice-over has the potential to succeed as a voice-over actor. However, it requires a willingness to risk your emotions, and the confidence to make a choice and commit to it. It also depends upon a willingness to study, practice, and face down your own fears as you let down the barriers between you and your emotions. Finally, you must develop the discipline to call upon those emotions and apply them with skill. That's hard work!"

EXERCISES:

Loosening-up Exercises.

These exercises are designed to relieve tension; to relax neck, face, and mouth muscles; and to open up the vocal range. They should be done while standing up, although most may be modified for use while sitting down. Consult your physician to make sure these exercises are for you, or ask your doctor to provide substitute exercises that will accomplish the same things. Never force your efforts past your level of tolerance, and stop immediately if you experience any pain or acute discomfort.

A. Inhale deeply through the nose, then exhale slowly through the mouth.

Do this three times.

B. Inhale slowly and deeply through the nose, filling the lungs to ninety-percent capacity. Feel the diaphragm being pushed out. Quickly inhale the last ten percent of air into the lungs and then let the breath out slowly, vocalizing an extended *ahhhh* sound during the entire exhalation.

Repeat once or twice.

C. Slowly, and without jerky movements, touch your left ear to your left shoulder, right ear to your right shoulder.

Repeat several times.

D. Drop your chin to your chest, then roll your head around in a loose, slow, 360-degree turn.

Reverse the direction of the roll and repeat.

E. Like a dog shaking its fur, shake your body from your shoulders on down.

F. From the diaphragm, repeat *Huh! Huh! Huh! Huh!* in short, powerful bursts.

G. Using the sound *ee*, bring your voice from its highest to its lowest pitch in a slow, sliding descent. Start by placing the voice in the very top of your head, then (slowly) bring it down into your forehead, nose, mouth, throat, chest, stomach, legs, down through your feet and out your toes.

Using the same *ee* sound, take the voice from its lowest to its highest pitch in a slow, sliding ascent. Make sure the voice is placed in the appropriate part of the body each step of the way and you will open up all your vocal areas. Repeat this exercise, using all the vowel sounds.

H. Make like a racing-car engine *brrrrrr!* and expel air through your lips. Do this several times. The vibrations will help to keep your lips loose and relaxed.

I. Pronounce the words *good blood, bad blood* very slowly, greatly exaggerating every sound. Keep your lips broad and loose. Say the words over and over, gradually increasing speed without losing clarity of diction.

Repeat this exercise, using the words *red leather, yellow leather, guttah, buttah*, and *buttah, guttah*. This will help you to warm up your mouth and ready your instrument for play.

BEGIN COLLECTING AD COPY.

Go through magazines and select ads with copy that appeals to you. We all have a picture of the image we project, so go ahead and choose copy that you can easily and naturally see yourself doing. (We have provided some original copy at the end of this chapter.)

At this point, we would recommend that you not use copy you have written. Being too familiar with the copy can hinder your ability to read copy written by other people, which is what you will be doing on an audition or job.

GET TO KNOW YOUR VOICE.

Select a piece of ad copy and record several readings of it without trying to change your natural voice in any way. Don't listen to your voice while you are recording—that's what playbacks are for.

Now play back your takes and make notes. Pretend you've never heard that voice before. Your assignment is to describe it in five words to someone whose only experience with the voice will be your description of it. Forget your lack of training for the moment—don't critique the reading—just determine what strikes you about that voice. What qualities would identify it to another person?

Also, listen for words you have difficulty pronouncing and work on them. You never know when they'll catch up with you. "I'd always had trouble saying the word 'aluminum,'" says Susan, "but I just ignored it. One day I auditioned for a job that would have meant a lot of money. I hadn't bothered to ask my agent what the product was. Naturally, the spot was all about aluminum, and I just couldn't get that word out of my mouth. I'd been careless and unprofessional, and now I was terribly embarrassed! I went straight home, determined to stay there until I could say 'aluminum' correctly."

Knowing what you do best is only the starting point. We want to enhance your natural voice with a few professional tips, then help you discover all the other people (voices) who are inside you, waiting for their turn at the mic. Here's the copy we promised you. Throughout the book and on the CD, we have written commercials using the names of products and companies that, to the best of our knowledge, are all fictitious. If any of our work contains existing copy, or the names of actual products or companies, our use of them was unintentional and coincidental.

LANDER'S LONG DISTANCE DIALING

Hello, Paul? How's college? ... This is
your mother--the one who did your laundry
for the past eighteen years. ... Right,
that one. You never call me. ... I know you
moved out only two days ago. Two whole days
and you never called me! ... "Expensive?"
Not if you have Lander's. ... Lander's
Long Distance Dialing. ... That's the phone
system your father put in so you could
call all your long-distance girlfriends for
practically nothing, remember? ... Right,
that one. Get Lander's, Paul, and call your
mother once in a blue moon. ... Lander's.
How do you think we could afford to send
you to college?

CREAHAN'S COMPUTER DATING

I thought computer dating was for the
much younger crowd. But then my daughter
Caroline talked me into signing up. Am I
ever glad she did! That's how I met Pete
(Cathy). He's (she's) wonderful and we have
so much in common. Now Pete (Cathy) and I
are going to talk my daughter into signing
up. After all, three is a crowd.

CALDE'S CREAMY LIP GLOSS

(Note: "Calde" is pronounced *caldee*, with
the accent on the first syllable.)

When my baby puts on Calde's Creamy
Lip Gloss, I can't resist kissing those
perfectly beautiful lips ... which means
she has to put on more Calde's Creamy Lip
Gloss ... which means I have to kiss her
again ... which means more Calde's Creamy
Lip Gloss ... which means another kiss ...
which means ... another perfectly beautiful
evening!

NUTS

Nuts--the fun food. Now that nut prices are down, buy them in quantity. And turn your home into a real nut house.

SHANNON'S BANDAGES

Oh boy, am I in trouble! Wait'll Mom sees my knees. I didn't mean to fall out of that tree. But I saw those birds and they were building a nest and I wanted to see it up close. I didn't know the branch was gonna break. Maybe Mom'll put that stinging stuff on my knees. I don't like that at all. But I do like what she puts on after. They're called "Shannon's Bandages." They're pretty and they make me feel good. (Calling.) Hey, Mom, do we have any Shannon's Bandages? I wanna feel good!

DONNA'S TRAVEL AGENCY

I love to travel. And I do a lot of it. Mostly for business. But when I'm not on a business trip, I travel for fun. And whether my trip is for work or play, I let Donna's Travel Agency make all my reservations. Their service is terrific. Sure, I could do it myself, but I deserve the best. I call Donna's Travel Agency.

MARG'S DINER

When I get the hungries, I head over to Marg's. It's this great little diner just down the road, and Marg herself does all the cooking. You just can't beat Marg's lamb curry or her pork chops, and her Yorkshire pudding is something to write home about. Even if your mom lives in England! So come on down to Marg's and treat yourself to some real good eating.

BOOKKEEPING BY JANE

When I started designing men's clothes, I did all my own accounting. But when the business really took off, I let all that bookkeeping stuff slide. Then the IRS came in and wanted to know what I'd been doing. "Creating," I told them. "Not good enough," they told me. So I got an accountant. Jane's her name and she comes in once a week to do my bookkeeping. Now my records are accurate to the penny, thanks to Jane. If you're honestly too busy "creating" to get to the books, call Jane. She'll keep you honest.

PARTIES BY NANCY

Want to give a special party and you don't know what to do? Nancy does. She's an expert when it comes to planning and organizing parties. For two or two hundred, Nancy knows exactly what to do to make your party very special. Just give her the date, time, and place, and she'll do the rest--from addressing and sending out your invitations, to planning the menu and hiring the caterers. Nancy. She knows how to make your party special because she's special.

AGING WITH THE VOICE

Here's an exercise where you can learn to explore and increase your age ranges with your voice. Remember that as your energy changes with age, so does your voice and pace. We can go from wide-eyed innocence, youthful enthusiasm, the eagerness of our 20s and 30s, the confidence of our 40s and 50s to the wisdom of our older years. You might nail some or even all of the ages or simply become more aware of how different attitudes affect your voice. Have fun!

(Infant crying ... to *goo's* ... to
laughing.)

I'm three years old and I love my mommy and
daddy and I like to ride my tricycle and
I like to feel the wind on my face and to
splash in puddles after it rains, but Mommy
says that's how you catch a cold.

Now I'm six and I'm getting dressed for my
first day of school, but I wanna know how
come I can't take my puppy with me? He's
going to be all alone and I'm gonna miss
him ...

You see, I'm ten years old and I ride my
bike to school and you can't come with us
'cause you're just a peewee. (Laugh). Come
on, you guys, let's get going!

Well, I'm thirteen and I just won this
spelling bee. Do you think that cute boy
(girl) noticed me up there on stage? I
think maybe I'll see if he (she) wants to
go out with me.

I'm seventeen years old and I'm going off
to college pretty soon. I'm real excited
about living on campus in a dorm--but I know
I'm gonna miss my family and friends back
home. I'm going for a Liberal Arts degree
and then ... who knows? What I really want
to do is write--be a great novelist.

Well, I'm twenty-five now and I'm working
for the town newspaper. I just wish I had
more exciting assignments than interviewing
the winner of a local chili cook-off.
I'm hoping to land a job with a big
metropolitan paper and cover real news!

I turned forty last week. It's hard to
believe time can pass so quickly. I'm

editor of my old hometown newspaper now,
and I feel like I've found the work I want
to do for the rest of my career. I've made
some big changes here ... The old *Tribune*
is now a vital, dynamic force in this
community--and I've boosted advertising
revenues 50%.

So, I retired last week at the ripe old age
of sixty. My kids have grown up now and
have their own families. They come to visit
us on holidays, and I stuff myself so full
of food (laugh) it just about fills me up
till they visit next time. I guess now's
the time to write that novel ...

My, my, I turned seventy-five last month.
The great-grandchildren bought me this fine
rocking chair. I guess they think I've got
nothing better to do than sit up here on
this creaky old porch thinking about the
old days. Well, I'm on my third novel now
and this one's about ...

Looking back, I figure I did most of what
I set out to do--though lots of times along
the way I wondered where life was taking me.
If I can give you just one bit of advice:
live life to the fullest every moment of
every day, and don't forget to stop and
smell the flowers.

2.

THE BASIC
PROCESS

*W*HAT WE CALL THE Basic Process is the foundation of voice-over excellence. If you read no other chapter, read—and remember—this one.

The best voice-overs are the ones that the consumers find most believable. Your listeners will not act on your recommendations unless they trust your voice. They will believe what you are saying only if you believe it. But in order for you to believe it, you must first know what is happening in the copy.

Ad copy is more than just a bunch of words strung together to promote a product. It is very much like a miniature play, with a beginning, a middle, and an end. One or more characters is involved, and it takes place at a particular time and place. You need to discover all those elements and more to act out the copy.

How do you get in touch with the reality of the copy? By using our Basic Process, which works every time: Focus, Visualize, and Commit.

1. FOCUS YOUR ENERGY ON DOING THE VOICE-OVER.

Minimize and/or eliminate all distractions. Turn off your cell phone or turn on the answering machine. Set up your real or mock music stand and mic. Make this uninterrupted time with yourself and your craft an appointment that cannot be cancelled, a real priority. Then you can concentrate all of your energy on the voice-over work in front of you and do your best work, knowing that everything you left behind will be waiting for you . . . whether you take fifteen minutes or twenty minutes or an hour.

2. VISUALIZE THE COPY.

Ask yourself certain questions about it. Sometimes the answers will be obvious; sometimes you will have to invent them. If you don't feel comfortable with an obvious answer, substitute one that works for you. Be specific in your choices and draw on your own experiences.

Select a piece of copy and go through the process with it, step-by-step. Move slowly and deliberately the first time so that the learning really sinks in. With practice, you'll pick up speed and proficiency.

Answer the following questions about the copy and do the process as directed:

A. Who is speaking?

Who are you: a mother, father, daughter, son, teacher, next-door neighbor, etc.? Remember to be very specific in your choice; don't just be a teacher, be a particular teacher. "Go inside and find one" (i.e., think back and pull a suitable one out of your memory or, later, out of your repertory of characters), and become that person.

How? Just as if you were getting dressed: Have a clear and detailed picture of the person in your mind, and then—item by item—put on his or her name, age, face, characteristics, mannerisms, clothes, and, especially, attitude.

Don't bypass this process and just try to imitate the voice. You will get bogged down in the concept of how it sounds—the result—and you'll start criticizing yourself while trying to do the voice. When that happens, you will lose that wonderful character you've created, as well as your potential for an excellent reading. If you successfully become everything else about a character, his or her voice will automatically come out of that process.

To whom are you speaking? Your aunt, your boss, your lover, etc.? Get a clear picture of the particular person for whom your words are meant. If you really talk to this person, you will automatically be talking to all your listeners. But the minute you lose this one person and address all your listeners, you will automatically sound like an impersonal announcer.

Make a choice (determine who you are and to whom you are speaking) and then record the copy. Don't play it back now, but make another choice and record the copy again. Repeat this process several times and then play back your takes. Notice how your voice changes as your choices change—as you become different people.

B. What is happening?

We don't talk to other people in a vacuum. Other things are going on at the same time. Are you washing dishes while the other person dries them? Having a last-minute conversation with your spouse while he/she is getting ready to go out jogging? Driving to work and talking things over with a member of your car pool?

Once you decide what is happening, you must also ask, "What is the pre-life?" Pre-life refers to what was going on with your character just before he or she starts to speak.

Were you out on a much-needed coffee break? Did your favorite team just win the pennant? Were you having dinner at a special restaurant?

You probably won't find this information spelled out in the copy, but the commercial itself may suggest what was happening, and your imagination must take it from there. Having a pre-life in mind will help you avoid cold, abrupt beginnings to your readings.

Now, make a choice as to who you are and to whom you are speaking, and also decide what is going on during and just prior (pre-life) to your take. Record the copy using these choices and notice in playback how another interesting layer has been added to your readings.

C. What time of day is it?

Is it an "early morning spot" that would call for a bright and cheerful delivery? Or does it take place late in the evening when a more laid-back approach would be appropriate?

Do it as several different people talking to different people at various times of the day, choosing a specific pre-life and action for each take.

Notice how much richer your readings are becoming as more dimensions are added.

D. Where is this happening?

How far away are the people you are talking to? Are they right next to you? Across the room? Across a breakfast table? Are you at a loud party where you would have to raise your voice to be heard? Are you at home, where you can occasionally lower your voice and still make a point? Are you in a park where you are competing only with the sounds of nature?

Be in various places and do several takes as different individuals talking to a variety of listeners at certain times of the day and, of course, select a specific pre-life and concurrent action for each take. In playback, see how yet another layer has been added to your performance.

E. Why am I doing this?

Whatever personal reasons you may have for doing voice-overs, the actor in you is really reading the copy to sell a product—the "newest," "fastest," "safest," "softest." But superseding all the adjectives we must believe—without reservation—that this product is the very best one there is. You know it; you just want someone else to know it, too.

Do several more recordings, experimenting with different choices as to who, what, when, where, and be very aware of the product and of its excellence. Play back the takes and notice how the name and the qualities of the product stand out—you have automatically (by staying in the process and out of the result) highlighted them.

3. COMMIT TO YOUR ANSWERS TO THE ABOVE QUESTIONS.

Once you have made your choices, stick to them throughout the entire recording. You can always go back and do it again another way. The sharper and clearer your picture of the copy, the sharper and clearer your reading will be—and the sharper and clearer your listeners' picture will be, too.

If you don't fully commit to all your answers, your readings will reflect this uncertainty and lack of conviction. And you will lose the trust of your listeners.

Now, play back all your takes. Notice again how they become richer and more interesting as more dimensions are layered into your readings. The copy really comes alive, doesn't it? Voice-over artist Brian Cummings says you must "build the copy into a living human being." He reads the copy, determines its message, and then gets a human relationship going. He emphasizes that a voice-over can't be just aural; in order for it to work, it must also be visual. After all, if you can't picture the person to whom you are speaking, how can you expect anyone else to?

Brian also advises us to remember that the person to whom we are speaking will have his or her own set of changing reactions—ranging from hostile skepticism to outright acceptance. While doing a reading, "see" that person's particular reaction at any given moment and your delivery will vary accordingly.

The Basic Process will never let you down. Using it allows you to make the copy your own little drama or comedy with its own life and vitality. Susan calls it "endowing the copy"—with that which makes it special or unique to you. And then your listeners will feel that it's special to them, too.

QUESTIONS

What if the person speaking is a person I don't have inside me?

If you can't find a particular person inside you, substitute someone else who can feel the same way about the product and about what is happening in the copy. Become that person and let him or her speak. This is a fail-safe technique that will always get you past this dilemma.

This copy is supposed to take place on a farm. I've never set foot on one. What should I do?

Again, use substitution. Determine whether your copy is a comfortable soft-sell (most likely true for a farm setting) or a more driving hard-sell. If soft (also called a "passive" commercial), picture yourself in your favorite quiet spot—the beach, a mountain cabin—wherever your special place is. Your delivery will take on a calm, relaxed quality that suggests rural peace.

If the copy is a hard-sell (also called an "active" commercial), imagine yourself in the boardroom of a Fortune 500 company, addressing a group of tough business executives, and your delivery will be charged with believable electricity.

I can't always figure out who the other person is.

Rather than addressing yourself to a vague, general audience, pick a particular relative or friend with whom a conversation always brings up a similar reaction. For example, Molly Ann's father has an incurable sweet tooth. When stuck for that "other person" to whom she must soft-sell something sweet, she always substitutes her dad.

On one audition Susan went through her entire repertory of friends and relatives and could not come up with the other person. Instead of giving up, she visualized a man—just an ordinary, all-American, middle-income guy—driving along in his car, listening to her voice on the radio, and spoke directly to him.

We recommend this technique only as a last resort. You use more energy "making up" a person than picturing one whom you know well and who is easy to visualize.

MOLLY ANN MULLIN

I've gone over this copy ten times and I still can't get a handle on it. Should I just keep on reading it over and over?

At this point, we doubt if even reading it fifty more times will give you the answers. You will also be under a time constraint in an audition or a job; you won't have the luxury of unlimited hours to study the text.

Voice-over writer and producer Larry Belling advises: "Here's a trick used by many voices. When they first look at a script, they read the last lines first. The last lines in the copy usually tell exactly what the writer is trying to say. This sets the tone and attitude for the entire reading of the spot."

That's good advice. Try reading the copy line by line from the bottom up. When you see where you are going, you'll have a clearer idea of how to get there. With this technique you'll know the end or high point of the text so you won't start your reading too high (at the same emotional level you would like to hit for the ending) and leave yourself nowhere to go with it.

Also try reading the copy a sentence or phrase at a time, and keep asking "what" or "why" for everything you read. Here's an example of what we mean. First, the text:

```
I could never understand why my brother
liked cottage cheese. It's always so runny
and lumpy. Then he told me his secret: he
buys Mullin's Small Curd Cottage Cheese. So
I went out and bought some. And you know
what? It's great--real smooth and creamy--
the way cottage cheese should be. Mullin's
Small Curd Cottage Cheese--it's the best!
```

Now, let's tear the text apart by asking "what" or "why."

What are the first few words of the copy? *I could never understand . . .*

You were confused about something. What couldn't you understand? *. . . why my brother liked cottage cheese.*

He liked cottage cheese; you didn't. Why not? Because it was *. . . always so runny and lumpy.*

If the cottage cheese you've tried is always runny and lumpy, why would anyone in his right mind—even your brother—buy some? It's *. . . his secret.* Ah hah! What is his secret? *Mullin's Small Curd Cottage Cheese.*

What's so special about Mullin's Small Curd Cottage Cheese? *It's great.*

Why is it great? Because it's *. . . real smooth and creamy—the way cottage cheese should be.*

You've finally found the answer to your cottage-cheese problems. What is the name of that wonderful product again?

Mullin's Small Curd Cottage Cheese.

Why Mullin's? Because *. . . it's the best!*

This quickie what/why process will begin to give you some clues to the emotions and action that are taking place in the copy. But it is only a beginning. Once you have a handle on what is going on (and why), you still need to bring the scenario to life using the Basic Process.

EXERCISES:

Practice and practice and practice the Basic Process until it becomes second nature to you.

Don't even think about going on to the next chapter until you have learned this technique. Other techniques and refinements you will pick up later. Right now, mastering the Basic Process is your priority. Without it, all your readings will sound alike—and that sound will be mechanical and lacking in conviction. Only by internalizing the Basic Process will you be able to instinctively and naturally give the most believable readings.

When listening to your work, practice being objective about that process.

Do not judge. Your attention will be on the last reading and will leave no room for the next. "That was a terrible reading!" is a negative judgment. "I didn't have a clear picture of who was speaking" is a constructive criticism. Constructive criticism has a positive, built-in indicator of what you need to do to make your reading better. In this case, the indicator tells you: "I need to have a clearer picture of who I am."

Practice not listening to your voice while you are recording.

Forget the picture of Gary Owens, hand cupped to his ear, delivering his wonderfully zany messages on *Laugh-In*. Gary was always and intentionally the "Announcer"; that was his character. But your characters are meant to be real people, and real people don't talk like that.

You can always tell when someone is listening to his or her own voice. Whatever picture that person started out with is lost as he or she focuses on the results (the sound). Consequently, the listeners' picture is also lost as the reading loses its internal life and falls flat.

Listen to radio and television voice-overs.

Decide which ones you like and which you dislike—and then figure out why you liked or disliked each one. Notice how a spot works because you can clearly see what the speaker is picturing. Also, notice how often the reasons a spot doesn't work tie in to factors you learned in the Basic Process. Remember, when you hear a line reading you particularly like, don't try to duplicate it. Identify the quality or attitude you like about it and learn to duplicate that. It is that attitude—and not the line reading itself—that can be adapted to any copy, and can go with you on any audition or job.

Turn the sound completely off when you watch a commercial on television.

Do all the voices (be all the characters) in that spot. Record your voice and make a video recording of the spot as well, if you have the equipment to do so. In playback, see if you were able to capture the various qualities and moods of the pictures.

Try writing your own commercial.

Start with a product you like and then build a text using the questions in the Basic Process to flesh out the scenario. Remember to give it a beginning, a middle, and an end. Keep it "tight." Don't use unnecessary words. Feature the name of the product and its selling points, and make it sincere and convincing. Either you will find you have a knack for writing ad copy (in which case you may want to write some material for your demo—see Chapter Seven), or you will begin to feel that crawling on your knees over cut glass is a lot more fun than writing copy. In that case you will be left with a healthy respect for the few good copywriters there are; they elevate the form to an art.

REFINEMENTS

I N THIS CHAPTER WE'LL polish your developing skills as we take a look at some of the more technical aspects of doing voice-overs.

Notice how people naturally speak. Their conversations are filled with sounds such as *um's, oh's, uh's,* etc. If you can add some of these to your readings, without having them sound forced or strained, your performance will seem even more relaxed and natural.

For example, record the line *This is delicious!* just as it's written. Now record it this way: *Mmmm, this is delicious!* Hear the difference? The line becomes more interesting and begins to acquire a personality of its own. In reading over your copy, you may come across certain words or phrases that you would like to stress or emphasize for a more natural delivery. Pat Fraley, one of the busiest and most talented voice-over artists around, developed the following techniques to highlight parts of his readings. He recommends that you practice each one alone to fully understand how it works, then go back and combine various techniques (which is what we do in normal conversation). Pat says that words or phrases may be given stress or emphasis by:

1. AN INCREASE OR DECREASE IN LOUDNESS.

This has to do with volume only. Keeping your voice in a monotone, record the phrase *I love you*, emphasizing the word *I*. Next, record the phrase, stressing the word *love*. Finally, record the line and hit the word *you*.

Play back the takes and notice how increasing the volume of the word *I* gives the phrase the meaning: *They* may not love you, but *I* do. Emphasizing the word *love* makes that verb-action very important and special: I don't just *like* you; I *love* you. When you emphasize the word *you*, a third meaning becomes apparent: I don't love someone else; I love *you*.

Repeat the exercise, using the phrase *They're here*, and this time decrease the volume of each word. Remember to keep it all monotone. In playback, hear how the readings differ in meaning. In one, a decrease in volume can indicate awe or fear as to who is here; in the other, location becomes important as we sense that they are very close.

As you go through these exercises, remember that one reading is not necessarily right or better than another. Our purpose is simply to let you experience how different readings may be obtained by using different techniques.

2. RAISING OR LOWERING THE PITCH.

Pitch has to do with the musical level at which we speak, the ups and downs our voices take in normal conversation. First, for contrast, record the phrase *For me?* in a monotone, without increasing or decreasing the volume of either word. Record it again, this time letting your voice go up in pitch on the word *me*. Hear how the second take says more clearly: *Gee, out of all the other people it could be for, is it really for me?*

Record the phrase *I'm sad* in a monotone. Now record it and let your voice register lower on the scale on *sad*, without prolonging the word itself. In playback, hear how much sadder your second take sounds.

3. INFLECTIONS AND STEPS.

These also have to do with musicality, but are generally used in connection with phrases longer than the ones we've been working with.

Record the phrase *That's the strangest thing I've ever seen* in a monotone. Now record it letting your voice go up and down in pitch (not volume) wherever it feels right. Chances are your inflections fell on the words *strangest* and *ever*. Try it again, hitting *that's*, *thing*, *I've*, and *seen*, and then try emphasizing various combinations of those words. Hear how the different emphases result in slightly different readings.

Steps work well when you are confronted with a long sentence that's packed with adjectives. You'll come across many of these since advertisers love to extol each and every virtue, real or imagined, of their products. These long strings of words are called "laundry lists."

Record the sentence *Now, these are brownies—fresh-baked, oven-warm, moist and chewy, and so chocolatey!* Let your voice go up in steps from one adjective to the next. Notice the excitement building in the reading as each adjective becomes more important and more appealing than the last.

4. PROLONGING OR SHORTENING THE DURATION OF A SYLLABLE, WORD OR PHRASE.

Record the phrase *I'm hungry* in a monotone. Now record it, prolonging the first syllable of the word *hungry*. Hear how much hungrier you are in the second take.

Record the phrase *I'm scared.* Then record it, prolonging the word *scared.* Hear how much more frightened you sound in the second take.

Record the sentence *It costs only one dollar and that's all.* Next, record it prolonging the phrase *It costs only one dollar.* Re-record it, prolonging the phrase *and that's all.* Notice how the second take calls attention to the amount of money it costs, while the third take emphasizes how small that amount really is.

Record the phrase *He's uptight.* Now record it, shortening the second syllable of *uptight.* Hear how much more uptight he is in the second take.

Record the phrase *You're right.* Now record it, shortening the word *right.* The second reading may sound a bit stilted, almost as if you resented the other person's being right.

Finally, record the sentence *We can't go in there—it's off limits.* Next, re-record it, shortening the phrase *We can't go in there.* Then record it, shortening the phrase *it's off-limits.* The second take sounds as if you were in a hurry to warn someone not to go in there. The third take calls attention to why you can't go in there—because it's off-limits.

5. PAUSING BEFORE, DURING, OR AFTER A SYLLABLE, WORD, OR PHRASE.

In normal speech, people often hesitate between words, phrases, and even syllables. A pause can be a powerful and dramatic addition to your reading, but first a word of caution: A voice-over pause must never be as long as a regular pause or your reading will sound as if it died. A voice-over pause automatically seems twice as long as a regular pause simply because there is usually nothing else going on at that moment to fill in the gap and hold your listeners' attention. All they hear is a lot of dead air.

With that in mind, record the phrase *Believe it!* as written. When you record it again, pause (briefly!) between the two syllables in *believe*. You'll hear how much more you want your listener to believe it.

Record the phrase *I love you.* Re-record it with a pause between the words *I love*. Notice how much more emotion the second take has.

Record the sentence *She used to work here, but that was a long time ago.* Now record it, pausing between the two phrases. The second take comes across with more nostalgia.

Pat cautions that, on an audition or a job, you will not have a lot of time to determine how each syllable, word, or phrase is to be read. Nor should that be your primary concern. Pat recommends that you first look at the emotional life of a line and then make a choice as to how you would like to read it.

And how do you determine what that emotional life is? By understanding what is going on in the copy—which brings us right back to the Basic Process.

A quick way to find natural stress points in copy is by doing another type of *what* exercise. Read the copy aloud, phrase by phrase, in character, and after each phrase ask yourself *what?* This *what* is not the *what did you mean?* of Chapter Two's what/why exercise, but simply a *what did you say?* as in: *Excuse me, I didn't quite hear what you said.* When your character then repeats each phrase, you will find yourself listening more closely to the copy and automatically stressing certain parts of it quite naturally.

When you have answered the Basic Process questions and made some choices concerning stress or emphasis for a particular reading, it is most helpful to have a system of marking the copy to remind you of those choices. Also, you may be given quite a bit of direction on a job and you need a quick way of noting those changes on your copy.

We will share our own copy-marking system with you, but we do so somewhat reluctantly. On the theory that you retain more easily that which you yourself create, we strongly recommend that you develop your own system. Use our notations only if you can't come up with your own symbols or if you feel perfectly comfortable with ours.

We have not developed a corresponding symbol for every technique of stress or emphasis that we discussed earlier. We have found that the following symbols have adequately met all our needs in marking copy. Should you wish to expand on our system, feel free to do so.

To indicate that a word or phrase is to be read more loudly, we draw a straight line under it:

```
I love you.
```

```
These cookies are great--did you make them?
```

We use an arrow to indicate inflection. To raise the pitch of a word or phrase, draw an arrow that points upward over it:

```
For me?
```

```
Try our six-dollar brunch--all you can eat!
```

To lower the pitch of a word or phrase, draw an arrow pointing downward over it:

```
I'm sad.
```

```
Come to New Zealand--enjoy quiet beauty.
```

In the sentence *That's the strangest thing I've ever seen,* suppose we wanted to put some inflection into the words *strangest* and *ever.* We would mark the words:

```
That's the strangest thing I've ever seen.
```

To indicate a pause before, during, or after a syllable, word, or phrase, we use one downstroke line to indicate the break:

```
Be|lieve it.
```

```
I|love you.
```

```
She used to work here, | but that was a long
time ago.
```

The punctuation that is marked on a piece of copy is not necessarily the punctuation you have to follow. More interesting and natural readings often occur when you ignore the given punctuation (or lack thereof) and pencil in your own. We sprinkle question marks and exclamation points liberally throughout copy, and we use parentheses to indicate word groupings we would like to make in our readings. Suppose a line is written:

```
My interview was in ten minutes and my
clothes were all wrinkled.
```

We would mark and read it:

```
(My interview was in ten minutes!) and (my
clothes were all wrinkled. ‖‖)
```

Our symbols for emotions are capital letters with circles drawn around them. We recommend that you mark emotions only when they go against the way a line would normally be read. For example, the line *I hate you!* would ordinarily be read with anger. In this case, there is no need to mark what is implicit in the line.

But suppose you are directed to read that same line as if you were afraid (i.e., against the text). We would put our symbol for afraid, (AF), slightly above and to the left of the line in question:

```
I hate you.
```

If an entire section is to be read against the text, we put a larger version of the symbol notation for the emotion in the margin next to the section.

We use the following signs to indicate some of the ways copy may be read. Before adopting our symbols, try developing your own. They'll feel more natural to you and come to mind more easily.

(LO) - loving (AN) - angry

(LI) - light (AF) - afraid

(TH) - threatening (HA) - happy

(SX) - sexy (HV) - heavy

(SD) - sad (WR) - worried

Now let's mark an entire piece of copy. First, take a look at the raw text:

```
When it comes to diets, I'm an expert.
There isn't one I haven't tried. But
nothing ever worked for me until I
discovered Diet Dinners. New Diet Frozen
Dinners satisfied my cravings for sinfully
delicious meals, and with so few calories,
I couldn't help but lose weight. If you'd
like to shed a few pounds painlessly,
try Diet Dinners. The tasteful way to a
slimmer you.
```

Here's the text as we would mark it for a reading:

(When it comes to diets, I'm an expert.)(There isn't one I haven't tried.)(But nothing ever worked for me until I discovered Diet Dinners.) (New Diet Frozen Dinners satisfied my cravings for sinfully delicious meals)(and with so few calories, I couldn't help but lose weight.)(If you'd like to shed a few pounds painlessly, try Diet Dinners.)(The tasteful way to a slimmer you.)

Most copy should be delivered with a smile on your lips. Record a piece of copy with and without a smile. Hear how much warmer the smile makes the copy. Even when the tone of the copy is serious, you can let that concern come through in your reading, but generally at some point there is room for a hopeful, problem-solving moment.

When Susan did a commercial for a medical pain center, she was directed to keep the tone serious and subdued, which she did. Yet at the end she let a little smile warm up the copy since the final message was one of hope: *Relief is available.*

A good way to keep your delivery fresh is to add the element of surprise to your performance. Discover something new each time you go through the copy, and read it as if you were pleasantly surprised to learn about that particular feature of the product. Your discovery becomes your listeners' discovery, and the attraction the product holds for you becomes theirs—which means they'll probably buy the product the next time they go shopping.

Another way to keep your readings fresh is to leave the chronological age of a character alone, but change his or her energy age. If your character is a seventy-year-old grandparent, for example, stay seventy but think twenty. Your listeners will hear a seventy-year-old speaking, but as if this were the first time he or she ever spoke those words.

Never let the end of a spot dissipate—which it will if you allow your voice to go down in volume or energy. Even if you feel that the last line should just comfortably fade away, punch it up anyway. It is the last thing your listeners hear, and it often contains the most important information about a product or the product's name itself. This especially applies to a soft-sell where you're holding your audience by a loose thread, which can break very easily. Your loss of intensity means their loss of interest. Always go for a strong finish to make a lasting impression on your listeners.

When delivering copy, Susan says to use your hands and body freely to become a particular character and to act out the play. If your character has a bad leg, for example, favor that leg at the mic. If your character has a habit of shaking his or her finger to make a point, do so . . . but don't stomp your feet, clap your hands, or hit any objects.

Just don't hit the mic! And don't turn your head away from the mic unless you are specifically directed to or you do so intentionally as a technique.

Also, if you are working a mic with one or more other people, courtesy and concern for their safety oblige you to confine your gestures and movements.

"I learned the hard way," says Molly Ann. "I was auditioning for a double and my partner was standing to my left. The spot was for an exciting getaway trip to a fun-filled island with wide, sweeping beaches and . . . you guessed it. When I hit 'wide, sweeping beaches,' I also hit my partner in the stomach. Actually, he took it quite well. Once he stopped gasping for air, he gently suggested that 'those wide, sweeping beaches might just as easily sweep off to the right, mightn't they?'"

Practice using a script stand for your copy. Adjustable music stands are excellent for this purpose. Holding the script in your hands is very unprofessional, and you will get paper noise as you record.

Headphones are fun to work with and you might want to spend some time getting used to them, but they are rarely used on an audition or job unless you are working with music.

Let's talk about mic technique. On an audition or job, the mic will often be your best and only friend. Practice getting so comfortable with the following techniques that you can simply relax and "romance" the mic when you do a reading.

In a class situation, you may be allowed to adjust the mic to your own height.

If so, mic courtesy calls for you to tighten the adjustment only to the point where the next person can loosen it with just two fingers.

On a job or an audition, never touch any of the equipment unless you are specifically asked to do so. And you won't be, unless it's a nonunion house.

Consistency. Unless your vocal highs and lows change drastically, always stay the same distance away from the mic.

Twelve to fourteen inches is recommended for a normal speaking voice.

The engineer must be able to pull a line from one of your earlier takes and cut it into copy from a later reading.

We asked the very talented head engineer at Salami Studios, Devon Bowman, if he would share his expertise on mic technique. He said, "Get comfortable with acting in front of a microphone. If you've never done voice-over work before, performing in front of a microphone instead of a group of people can be a little intimidating. The more you play in front of a mic, the more natural it will become. It's stressful enough going on your first audition, let alone being put into an isolation booth with a mic in front of you and being asked to perform— don't make it more so by not being used to working with a mic."

Devon also contributed the text and diagrams for the following five pages on mic technique, noise, and booth protocol.

Microphone Handling.

The equipment you will use and be exposed to is delicate. The microphone stand, music stand, and shock mount for the microphone itself never need to be over-tightened; always use a gentle touch. The threads on these parts can be stripped easily.

Having said that, you will never be asked to handle the equipment yourself in a professional recording session. If the mic placement creates a problem for you where you cannot see your script, do not adjust the microphone yourself. You don't want the responsibility of replacing a microphone or mic stand. Let the engineer know that there is an issue and they will be more than happy to accommodate.

Microphone Technique.

If you were to extend your pinky finger and your thumb in a "hang-loose" gesture, this will give you a good starting distance that you should have between the mic and your mouth. But given genetic differences, this is only a rule of thumb. Okay, bad pun, but you get the idea.

With this starting distance in mind, try not to vary too drastically from it, either front to back or left to right. Still feel free to act and get into character, but drastic swings or turns of the head will cause your voice to sound "off-mic" or "off-axis." The goal is to maintain a consistent sound quality so that if your performance needs to be edited together from different takes, there will be little or no change in continuity.

There are a couple of exceptions to this rule, however. If you are going to do a "stage whisper" or the character is naturally soft-spoken, adjust your distance closer to the mic. If you are going to project strongly, or yell, back off the mic, but do so in moderation—going too far will cause your voice to sound off-mic. Generally all you need to do is lean back in your chair or stool to about twice the distance from your starting position or look off-axis slightly (about forty-five degrees). Also, be aware of what your hands are doing. If your character needs to yell a line, don't cup your hand next to your mouth as this will alter the sound of

proper placement of a typical dynamic style microphone
(Shure SM58) using a desk stand
note: arrow shows angle of reflection away from the microphone

proper placement of a typical condenser style microphone
(Neumann U87 or TLM103) using a floor stand and boom.
note: arrow shows angle of reflection away from the microphone

your voice. In general, hand movements close to your mouth or to the mic will create a similar problem.

Get to know the "proximity effect" of a mic. This effect is best described by listening to trailer and promo V.O. You can hear a distinct richness in the low end of the performer's voice. This proximity effect is created by coming in tighter on the mic, which will naturally pick up the low end of your voice. Each mic is unique and has a slightly different proximity effect and how close to the mic it begins to occur. So play around with proximity effect and get to know all the other techniques for using a microphone. After all, the better you know how to use a microphone and these techniques, the better you will sound.

Pop Filters.

If you put your hand in front of your mouth and make a *p* sound, you can feel the amount of air coming out of your mouth into the imaginary microphone (your hand). This sudden burst of wind into the mic creates an undesired effect called a "pop"—the sound of which is quite similar to that of a gust of wind passing by your ear. To control this natural effect, pop filters were invented. Back in the day before these were manufactured, engineers would make them by hand out of a wire coat hanger and pantyhose by taking the coat hanger and making a loop at one end and wrapping the other end around the mic stand, then slipping the stockings over the loop and placing the loop between the performer's mouth and the mic. But now there are companies that make various types of pop filters.

There are two basic types: pop filters and wind-socks or muffs. Pop filters look just like you'd think from the description above— they have a clamp that affixes them to the mic stand and a flexible neck that allows you to place the screened loop in front of the mic. Wind-socks and muffs are basically hollowed-out chunks of foam that slip over the top of the mic and are a more extreme way of controlling pops. But as you can imagine, any time you put more of anything between you and the mic, whether it's a foam wind-sock, your hand, or a piece of paper, it's going to alter the sound quality of your voice. Because of this, I prefer to use a pop filter instead of a wind-sock.

Whistling, Plosives, and Sighs . . . Oh, My!

If your character is in a scene and is whistling a tune or needs to sigh heavily, understand that these effects require a lot of air to be expelled out of your lungs and directed at the microphone. Doing so right into the microphone will create a wind-pop similar to what we talked about above. To avoid this, simply turn your head a little off-mic and that will take care of everything. Any time your mouth is completely closed and then is opened with a hard consonant (b, c, k, p, or t) it will create a small burst of wind called a plosive. Pop filters will most times take care of these effects. In situations where they do not, simply tuck your chin down slightly, and only for the duration of the consonant, as if you were to nod your head "yes."

Mouth Noise.

Everyone's mouth is different. Mouth shape and mechanics, diet, speaking for a long time, and nervousness can all contribute to how noisy a performer's mouth is. The basic reason for this is dry mouth, and the resulting sounds are small clicks. One way to prevent mouth noise is to watch what you eat before going into a session or while on break. Foods high in dairy content, coffee, and soda should be avoided. There are many performers who practically live on coffee and are lucky enough not to have these problems. However, it's always best to have fresh water with you and take a drink every so often. It will help with dry mouth and will keep your throat wet. And make sure it is room-temperature water, because refrigerated water tends to constrict your vocal chords. Also, green tea with honey is great for coating your throat if you are going to be using your voice a lot.

Clothing Choices.

That starched shirt may look sharp for an on-camera test, but leave it behind while working in front of a mic. Be conscious of your clothing choices. Nylon windbreakers and jackets, starched shirts, silk blouses, even nylon track-pants can all make noise. I've had performers taking off their shirts to do the job—never the pants, though, and I would like to keep it that way. If you are wearing a baseball cap, either turn it around or remove it. The bill of the cap creates a similar effect to that of cupping your hand at the side of your mouth, otherwise known as phasing. Jewelry can make noise also. Chains, zippers, bracelets, earrings—even keys and change in your pocket—can all make noise, so remove any potential noisemakers before getting down to work. I had a situation once with a very well-known actor whose undoubtedly very expensive watch was "ticking" loud enough for me to hear it. I asked him to remove it because of the sound, to which he shot me a dubious look and asked, "You can hear THAT?" and held his watch up to the microphone. I told him I could, and he kindly removed the offending watch. Only to be caught again wearing the watch after taking a break, and having to remove it again.

Cell Phones and Pagers.

Obviously, having your cell phone ring while in the recording studio is poor form, so turn it off. And by that I don't mean to put them on silent. I mean turn them all the way off. The reason for this is that even if the phone or pager is on "vibrate only" that vibration can still be picked up by the microphones. Yes, they are that sensitive. Also, there is an initial signal that is sent to the phone that is picked up by the equipment in the studio, which will ruin the performance being recorded at that moment.

Choosing a Microphone for You.

If you ever decide to purchase a microphone for home use, keep in mind that just as everyone's voice is different, every mic is different. When shopping for a mic, test out many different brands, and use the mic techniques we've talked about to determine how well it responds to your voice. It can be an expensive purchase, but think of it more as an investment and take the time to make a smart choice. Remember: test, test, test.

Microphones can be broken up into two basic categories: dynamic and condenser. Basically, dynamic mics do not require power to run them, tend to be more road-worthy, and can handle higher volume levels. Typically you see dynamic mics used on drum kits, guitar amps, and in concerts. Condenser mics require external power, called "phantom" power, which is usually supplied by the mixing console or a mic pre-amplifier. These microphones are generally more delicate both in terms of road-worthiness and volume-level handling. But without a doubt they are the only choice for capturing your voice. Once you purchase your own microphone, take care how you store it. Too much humidity can be a problem, as can airborne particulate such as cigarette smoke and dust. Always use two hands while carrying your microphone. One small drop can ruin the electronics inside. After long-time use it is not uncommon to take your microphone for a professional cleaning. Once you get it back, it will sound "brand new."

WRONG

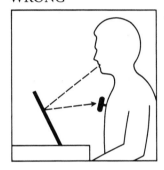

RIGHT

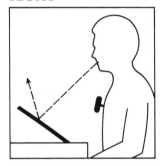

WRONG

RIGHT

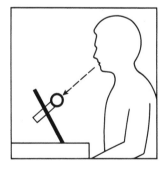

QUESTIONS:

Without getting too technical, how are commercials made?

Nicholas Omana says: "Representatives from the advertising agency and/ or from the client company itself bring me a spot. I get as much information as possible from the client so I'll know exactly what he or she is trying to say in the copy." (What the copy says and what the client thinks the copy says are often two different things.) "We cast the spot. Sometimes clients already have certain artists in mind or 'on hold,' and we have to use them. Usually it works out, especially if the talent is the regular spokes for the product.

"We have a recording session. We begin with a run-through, which gives everyone a chance to hear the latest rewrites and to prepare for the actual takes. The engineer adjusts the mic and sets levels on the equalizer to roll off or boost certain frequencies.

"We do a take. Even if the first take is a buy, we do several more right away for backup protection. First-take buys are rare; clients usually want to hear the copy read several different ways so they'll have something to choose from.

"We do even more takes over a longer period of time, especially if rewriting is still going on or there are technical problems.

"Once the talent has laid down the voice tracks to everyone's satisfaction, the artist goes home and the major part of the technical work begins. In post [post-production], the engineer mixes down [combines] the various voice, music, and sound-effects tracks into a final product."

How much of the technical stuff do I really need to know?

Not a lot. Just enough to do your job professionally. Most of it you'll get from this book and, if anything else sparks your curiosity, you can always ask an expert. Just don't ask them when they are working. Like you, technical people don't take kindly to folks who break their concentration.

Nicholas makes an interesting point: "If you know too much, it can actually be a handicap or a distraction. Particularly if you have done production work yourself. If you're hired as talent, do that and nothing more. When you go into the studio, let it all go. Relinquish responsibility and let everybody do their own jobs."

How long do sessions last?

Anywhere from five minutes to several hours. Producers aren't asking you to do more takes for their health. They have legitimate reasons—technical problems, ongoing rewrites, hard-to-satisfy clients, etc. But they are always aware that time is money and the clock is ticking.

Every hour spent in a recording session means at least two hours of post to complete the job. That's why the producers don't want to keep you around any longer than they have to. Once you go, they've still got a lot more expensive work to do.

What happens if I'm in a session and there's just too much copy to read in the specified amount of time?

First, make sure that the problem is with the copy and not with you. One of the exercises in this chapter will have you working with a stopwatch to develop exact timing.

Unless the problem is clearly in the script, it falls on you to bring that copy in on time. Nicholas explains what happens if your readings are too long or too short:

"If you are under, the client yells at the producer: 'You owe me more time—I paid for it!' If you're over, the producer yells at the client: 'You're getting free time and I'm paying for it!'"

I could probably bring the copy in on time if I quit breathing.

Don't do that. The world would be minus one very special voice-over artist. Ask the engineer or producer for help, just as we asked John Westmoreland for help with this question.

"If your breathing actually interferes with your reading of the copy (either because the copy itself is too long or because you have been mic'd 'breathy'), it is sometimes better to slow down just a bit and give yourself a small pause before and after your breathing. Keep the copy itself rolling along at a fairly good clip.

"In post, the breaths themselves can be taken out and the timing corrected. We can cut you down into something inhuman (because you're not breathing), but you'll sound perfectly fine because people accept unrealistically short audio pauses that they'd never buy if you were on camera."

EXERCISES:

Practice working with background music and/or sound effects.

If you have access to two audio recorders, put various background sounds and music on one, then play it while superimposing copy on the second machine. Although you will probably not often record over music or other sound, this exercise will familiarize you with the process.

Learn to work with a stopwatch.

Practice exact timing in delivering copy. A thirty-second spot should come in at exactly thirty seconds. Air time is expensive and must be precisely filled. Often music and sound effects are added to a spot after you have recorded it, and the timing is critical.

Work with a stopwatch until you develop an internal stopwatch. The true professional can shave a second off a spot on command, without even glancing at a clock.

"One thing my DJ work gave me," says Nicholas Omana, "was an internal clock. I didn't have to learn timing when I started studying voice-overs. I already had a stopwatch in my head."

Before we get into the next chapter, where you will be developing a number of characters, it's time to ask—particularly if you are a non-actor—whether you are feeling at all self-conscious about becoming another person. If so, this exercise will help you get past that feeling. While standing, read a short piece of copy, then put it aside. Observe your reactions to the readings. What are you doing? What are you feeling? In a stream-of-consciousness flow, record your thoughts and observations in a very loud voice. Do this for a good three minutes. Here's what one student said:

> Well, I'm just standing here, shifting from one foot to the other. Maybe I should be crushing grapes. . . . I feel funny without a piece of paper in my hands. I've got my hands at my sides. Now they're clasped in front of me. . . . I'm not used to staring at four walls—especially four walls that are staring right back at me. . . . I wonder what it would feel like to be on a stage—like the Shubert, where I saw *Cats*. I'd probably drop dead in front of that many people. . . . Now I'm running one hand through my hair. What am

I looking for—lice? . . . I think I'll take my jacket off. It's getting
pretty warm in here. There—it's off. . . . Wouldn't you know? The
phone's ringing. Well, tough. The machine'll get it. . . . There—the
machine got it. . . . I've got to come up with a new message—
nobody believes that I'm "not here right now." They know damn
well I'm here; I'm just not picking up. Everybody knows I'm here
because I'm only on Chapter Three. They know that if I were on
Chapter Ten, I'd be out auditioning somewhere. Yeah, and if I
were out auditioning somewhere, I'd be scared to death. . . . Gee,
it's quiet when the phone's not ringing. . . . I'm picking up my
jacket again. Why am I doing that? I just took it off. Must be
nerves. Susan says everyone has nerves. I'll bet she doesn't. Nerves
of steel. Professionals don't get nervous, do they? Maybe they do.
Maybe they're human, after all.

When you've pretty well run down your feelings, immediately grab
that piece of copy and read it aloud—in character. You will find that
this exercise not only raises your energy level, it also gets rid of the
inhibitions that stand between you and the text, thus making you one
with the copy.

This exercise will also work for you on an audition or in any situation where you feel uncomfortable. Always talk your feelings out loud
if at all possible, but at least get in touch with your fears and they will
often shrink from the size of Mount Everest to that of a speed bump.

**If you've stuck to hard-sell commercials up till now, pick a soft parent/
child spot and get comfortable doing it.** If you tend to do soft-sells, practice recording more active commercials. When that phone call comes for
an audition—for a job that means $$$$—you can't tell them: "Diapers?!
Are you kidding? All I know how to sell are big rigs and bulldozers!"

Don't place limits on your learning or you will only limit your range
and your career. Other people try to limit you enough anyway—don't do
it to yourself.

4.

OTHER VOICES

B Y NOW, YOU ARE fairly well acquainted with a few of your characters. When asked to do a teacher, you become that particular teacher you learned to visualize in Chapter Two, etc. But what about all the other people still inside you? How do you reach them? How do you develop other voices?

As Pat Fraley says, "The number of voices you do is actually the number of characters you do." And the more voices you do, the more chances you will have of working. For Pat, the bottom line is developing and keeping different characters, and in his wonderfully analytical and organized fashion, he has designed an excellent system for doing both.

The following are Pat's exercises to discover other voices. You may find that only one works for you, or maybe you will be comfortable doing all five. But try them all. As you do this process, something interesting will begin to happen. Since by now you are proficient in doing the Basic Process, the new sounds you make will automatically trigger more than just new voices for you—new people will come out of your imagination to go with those new voices.

1. IMPRESSIONS.

Run through a list of stars and record your impressions of how they speak. With the help of an objective friend who has a good ear, decide which impressions are closest to how a given star actually sounds. Keep the very best ones in your repertory of can-do impressions.

Don't discard the less-than-excellent ones; they might be of service to you. Listen to them carefully and you just might discover other interesting voices in there, characters worth keeping.

Susan adds: "Don't stop at the gender barrier. If you are a man, do female celebrities, and if you are a woman, by all means do male celebrities. Out of these reaches on your part will come the most interesting character voices. For example, a man imitating Julia Child will produce a unique character, while a woman imitating John Wayne will also come up with someone different and special. This takes you way beyond the realm of straight spokes and enriches your stable of characters."

2. CENTER WORK.

Turn on your recorder and just let it run while you do this physical exercise.

Center your attention on a particular part of your body and talk from there. How? Imagine there is a thorn in your nose. Focus only on that thorn and start talking. Talk about how it feels to have that thorn up your nose. It doesn't matter what you say; it's the feeling that counts. Later, in playback, you will probably hear a pinched, nasal, agitated voice.

Next, imagine there is a huge, soft sponge in your stomach. The sponge soaks up everything in sight and keeps getting bigger and bigger. Focus only on that sponge and start talking from the feeling of it. Have you discovered a rolling, heavy, slow kind of character?

Notice how the process of choosing and speaking from a center will automatically result in different characters as well as different placements for your voice. Go all out with this exercise. Work on placing that voice everywhere from the top of your head to the tips of your toes. See how many characters you can add to your repertory.

3. INANIMATE OBJECTS.

Keep that recorder running as you look around the room and select particular objects. Become those objects. Start describing yourself as each one and how it feels to be that object.

Let's say you picked that old armchair right in front of you. Become the chair and start talking. You might say something like *I am a very old armchair. My upholstery is fading and I'm sagging all over because I'm old and so many people have sat down on me. I don't mind them sitting down, but I do mind when they put their feet up on me. Nobody would dare do that when I was new!* Later, in playback, you might find you've discovered a crotchety, peevish, old character.

Try being a ceiling lightbulb. When Molly Ann did this exercise, her lightbulb said, *I'm a bedroom ceiling light. Those people down there don't know it, but I'm watching them. I'm watching everything they do. Oh, wow! You wouldn't believe what they're doing now! They could get arrested for that! Hey, wait! Wait! Don't turn me off! I can't see anything if you close my eye!* This gave Molly Ann a nosey voyeur type of character (as well as a reputation she's having trouble living down).

Another variation to this exercise is to listen to the sounds around you: a motorcycle, a car alarm, a creaking door. Now, try to imitate the sound that the object makes. Do it until you feel like you have a handle on it: the noise, the rhythm, the vocal placement. Then, after making that sound, try to talk in that placement or sound quality, in that same rhythm, using that inanimate object to source a unique character. A creaking door could become a great older person, or someone who is cranky; a motorcycle could be gruff; a car alarm could be a high-pitched or more excitable person.

4. ANIMALS.

Become various animals, and talk about which animal you are and how it feels. Be a monkey, for example, and chatter away into your recorder. You probably will get a small, nervous, twitchy kind of character.

Next, be a gorgeous, long-haired cat and see if you don't come up with a serene, languid, and dignified character. Susan suggests you try something similar to her inanimate object exercise. Make the sound of a certain animal and let a voice come right out of that sound. Susan did this with the *baaaa* of a sheep and got a wonderful Katharine Hepburn-like character.

5. IMITATING FROM THE TELEVISION AND RADIO.

Find different kinds of shows and record about ten to fifteen minutes of each. Next, try to imitate every sound and voice you hear on each particular program. Do this for ten to fifteen minutes at a time as it can be very demanding. This is an excellent way to create and expand your roster of characters as exact imitations or as impressions with your own unique spin.

Here is an example of Pat's character classification sheet to catalogue each character that you come up with.

1. Character's Name.

Always name your characters. If you do a terrific Bob Newhart impression, you would probably want to name that character Bob Newhart. If the character is one you have created from a less identifiable source, invent a name that you will immediately associate with that character. To name the dignified, serene voice of that gorgeous, long-haired cat you worked with earlier, you might want to call her *Cat*herine The Great or him *Scat*man The Magnificent—whatever, as long as it identifies that character to you.

2. Source of the Character.

How did you find the character? Knowing your source can help you recall the character as you recall the process by which you found him or her.

3. Vocal Elements.

Pat further categorizes his characters by determining the following seven vocal elements for each one.

Before you do this process, go through the elements and categorize your own natural voice. This is a more methodical and refined approach than we used in Chapter One, where you used a few adjectives to describe the sound of your voice to another person. It is also the best place to start, since other voices are actually extensions of your own voice, which is altered by every change made in each of the vocal elements.

A. Pitch.
This has to do with the musical note of the voice. Is the voice high or low? It can also be labeled tenor, soprano, bass, or alto.

PAT MUSICK

B. Tone.
Tone refers to the quality of the pitch. It can be rough, nasal, sexy, sloppy, metallic, harsh, gravelly, clear, etc.

C. Fluctuation.
How much fluctuation is there between the highs and the lows? If the fluctuation is very high, the voice will go up and down quite a bit. If it is very low, the voice will be a monotone.

D. Tempo.
Does the character speak slowly or quickly? A nervous little monkey would speak with a much faster tempo than a big, lumbering polar bear.

E. Rhythm.
Is the speech syncopated, lilting, pedantic, etc.? This is not the same as tempo; the character can speak with a slow tempo, yet maintain either a lilting or a syncopated rhythm.

JENNIFER DARLING

F. Placement.
Where is the voice physically located? Speak as the character and imagine where that voice is coming from. Be very specific. Does the voice seem to come from the back of the throat, the tip of the nose, or is it closer to the bridge of the nose?

G. Gate (Dialect).
Does the character have an accent? If so, is the dialect heavy or light?

Dialects are usually the last refinement you add to a voice. Pat recommends that you always start with your own voice when you practice a dialect. Once you have the accent, then you can layer it onto other voices you are experimenting with. (We will have more to say about dialects later in this chapter.)

4. Key Phrase.
This is a wonderful, quick way to get back into character. Write a phrase that is very typical of each character. The Dignified Cat might say: *I can't be bothered right now—I'm busy being beautiful.* With practice, you can get

to the point where you won't need to put on the character item by item
as we did in Chapter Two; simply say the key phrase and you will be
that character.

5. Notes.

Add any and all information that helps you to identify the character. If
your character comes from the image of an old armchair in your grandpar-
ents' home, make a note of that. If your character has certain mannerisms,
list them. One woman we know is a good amateur artist. She makes a
little sketch of each of her characters as a visual aid to identifying them.

Wherever your new characters come from—once they do show up,
don't let them go! Make friends with each and every one. Name them, categorize them, and know everything there is to know about them. Practice
being them until you can quickly and easily get into each character.

Let's talk about accents for a moment. How do you get an accent?
Voice-over artist and director Philip L. Clarke, a recognized expert in
accents and dialects, says that perhaps the worst place to go looking for
accents is old movies. Although you can find a few actors who were actually from other countries and who had genuine foreign accents, most
actors vocalized what they thought a particular accent should sound like.

Philip emphasizes that accents "must be authentic. The more authentic
they are, the more believable you are. But don't make the accent too thick
or you'll lose your audience. The idea is to 'get' the full accent, then 'bring
it down' to the point where you can be understood." And where do you
get the accent? If you are not able to go to the actual locale, then seek
out people who are from the region or country whose accent you wish to
learn. Airports, ethnic restaurants, and cultural centers are excellent places
to find these people. Ask them questions; get them talking; then listen to
them speak. Watch their mouths to see where sounds are placed. Record
them if you can for later reference. Philip feels that most dialect recordings on the market are a less satisfactory way of learning accents because
they can't give you the visuals of an accent—the sound placements and
especially the mannerisms that accompany the actual language.

Mannerisms? Most definitely! As Philip says: "It is not enough just
to 'do' an accent. You also must create a body for that accent to live in."
For credibility's sake, never let an accent come out of your mouth without
having one of your characters do the talking.

Keep mimicking the speakers you are studying until you know exactly how they would say something without first having to hear them say it. And practice! One of Philip's favorite exercises is to take a magazine (*Time*, for example) that carries articles about many different countries, and to read each article aloud, using that country's particular accent.

Animation work generally calls for caricatures of accents as opposed to the more realistic accents used in commercials. But, as Philip points out: "In either case you must be completely believable in terms of authenticity of accent and character."

It is not unusual for directors to ask to hear another voice. Advertising people often ask for a spokesperson. All they really want is to hear one or more of your characters speak—as living, breathing, real people. This means that you must be so familiar with your characters and their attitudes that you can comfortably ad lib for a minute or so as each one. Just remember to keep it natural—believe who you are, and they will believe it, too.

MICHAEL SHEEHAN

5.

TAGS AND DOUBLES

TAGS ARE A FEW words or short phrases that either end a piece of copy or stand alone to identify and describe a product. "Coke is it"; "Western Airlines—the only way to fly"; and "Seven-Up—the Uncola" are examples of tags.

If you are called on to do a tag, consider yourself blessed. You have a chance to make some quick, easy money. If you are union (we'll talk more about unions in Chapter Ten) and are hired for a session, even if it's five minutes, you will still be paid as if you had worked a full session.

Tags are deliberately written to make a lasting impression on the listener. And that is how they should be delivered. Tags are always "punched," never "pushed" or "forced." Pitch may drop in a reading for dramatic effect, but not the energy or volume. We'll give you some tags to work on at the end of this chapter.

Up to this point, we have kept the focus on "singles" or one-person spots. Now it's time to consider "doubles," or two-person spots. The beginning of our Introduction to this book was much like a double, with both of us speaking as one person to you, the other person in the spot.

Since doubles are often done on radio or television but are seldom published in magazines, we will provide some two-person spots for you to study and use for practice.

Here's a double for the fictitious Bingham's Furniture Store.

NEPHEW	Well, how do you like it?
AUNT	This is your new apartment?
NEPHEW	Well, it's new to me. It's my very first apartment.
AUNT	There's a hot plate on top of the television set!
NEPHEW	Yes. I call that my kitchen.
AUNT	What's this? Oh, a walk-in closet.
NEPHEW	That's the bathroom, Aunt Marian.
AUNT	Oh, dear! Where's the bedroom?
NEPHEW	You just sat down on it.
AUNT	You sleep on the couch?
NEPHEW	It's a queen-size sofa bed from Bingham's Furniture Store.
AUNT	From Bingham's? Well, there's hope for this place after all!

Notice that, just like a single, the double is actually a miniature play. It has a beginning, a middle, and an end: Aunt Marian comes into her nephew's new apartment; she starts discovering the features of the apartment and becomes more and more troubled by her findings; at last there is peace when Aunt Marian learns that her nephew is sleeping on a Bingham's sofa bed.

There is no "secret" to doing doubles. Treat them as you would a single—understand the copy, visualize it, become your character, and deliver the lines. But remember this important difference between doubles and singles: In a double, you have the person to whom you are speaking actually standing right next to you. Since the dialogue is between the two of you, listen and react to what your partner's character says.

Furthermore, we usually have the obligation to keep up the pace . . . often it is read with almost an overlap with the other actor. As Roger Scott says, "We mustn't ever let the feather fall to the ground." That is to say, DON'T let the energy lag. Also, be sure to pick up your cues . . . start your line immediately after the other actor finishes his or hers. Often, the actors in a group read are cast for contrast—one person who is, say, sweeter or warmer contrasting with one who is higher energy and quirky, etc. Always read the specs (character descriptions) and ask the casting director or booth director (if you are reading at your agency) what they have in mind for each character, then make your choices and fulfill their intention. Doubles and group reads often allow us an opportunity to embellish the copy a bit, to add a word or two, a sigh, perhaps, or finish with an appropriate little tag or exit line that might be memorable.

Tom Kenny & Susan Blu

The very best acting really isn't "acting" at all—it's based on reality and what we do naturally, listening and reacting to other people. We suggest that you meet regularly with a few voice-artist friends to work on doubles and even multiples. You'll acquire skill in this area, plus you will give and get immediate feedback on your performances.

Always work with your partner as a fellow artist, too. On an audition, you may be competing for a job, but do not compete with your partner during the reading of your particular spot. The more the two of you cooperate and are mutually supportive, the more you will enhance your own readings. Working doubles simply means that you are playing another game—one that can be contagiously exciting and a whole lot of fun. All you need is a partner who has an imagination and a willingness to play like a child—abandoning every inhibition and committing totally to a particular character.

Ask your partners how they "see" the copy. If your partners' feelings are in agreement with your own, your work is already half-done. If you have the time to do a quick run-through with your partners without disturbing anyone, do so. Step outside for privacy, if you want. If you don't have the time, or if your partners prefer not to do a run-through, just keep your character firmly in mind. Be ready to commit to that character and to your picture of the copy when the time comes to record it. Remember, too, to listen to your partners, so you can at least react to them.

If your partners have no particular thoughts as to how a piece of copy should be read, describe your own visualization of what is going on in the text. The more clearly you paint the picture, the greater the chances your partners will see it too and be able to hold that same picture in mind when recording.

Sometimes your partners will have a completely different idea of what is going on. Always give them the courtesy of hearing them out. Perhaps they have thought of something that hadn't occurred to you—something that would make your readings terrific. But if you can't honestly agree with their concept, ask them if they would be willing to try it your way in a practice run-through. Sometimes other voice-over artists need to read copy a particular way in order to "hear it" and get a feel for it.

When you can't persuade your partners to do it your way and there is a great deal of resistance on their part, don't force the issue. This will only cause resentment and animosity, which will inevitably show up in your readings. A mic never lies.

Chances are that difficult partners are not deliberately being difficult; they may have had a rough day, or they just

LEA VERNON AND GREG CALLAHAN REHEARSE THEIR LINES FOR A "DOUBLE."

may be arm-wrestling with a bad case of nerves. But don't risk picking up their negativity. Smile encouragingly, then move away to a place where you can keep your own positive energy intact. You can always ask the director for guidance once you get inside the studio.

When you do get in to record, don't be concerned if your partners give a poor performance. Your concern and worry will only use up the energy you need for your own reading. And even if your performance is up to its usual high standards, your partner's "off" readings will make yours sound that much better.

Remember basic mic techniques, too. In the unlikely event you are sharing a microphone, mic courtesy calls for you to do just that—share the mic. Only a nonprofessional hogs the microphone. Deliver your lines to your partner, but do not turn your head away from the mic to do so.

To make your doubles sound completely natural, use what people do in their everyday conversations. When one person speaks, the other reacts. Add sounds to the text, as audible reactions to what your partner is saying. A mic won't capture the skepticism of a raised eyebrow, but it will catch the *hmmm* you can interject into a reading. Before one person completely finishes speaking, the other usually jumps right in and contributes his or her two cents to the conversation. Practice overlapping (but be careful not to "step on") lines, and watch out for long pauses, which will sabotage even the best readings with dead air.

Here are some more doubles for you to practice with a partner. Take turns doing the different parts, changing the text and/or the sex of any given speaker to accommodate your readings. Either one of you may be the Announcer; just remember, the Announcer is always another, completely different, character from the speakers.

(FROM OFF) means the line is to be said slightly to one side of or back from the mic so the speaker will seem to be in another location.

(MOVING OFF) means the speaker is to deliver the line while moving away from the mic, thus indicating that he or she is leaving the room.

Record all your readings, and give each other detailed, constructive critique. Finally, enjoy the game. Have a ball starring in all sorts of mini-plays, endowing each piece of copy with its own very special life.

ROMANO'S PIZZA

CUSTOMER   I'd like a pizza, please.

SERVER   We got chicken and spareribs.

CUSTOMER   No, I'd really like a pizza.

SERVER   How about fish filets or a hamburger?

CUSTOMER   All I want is a pepperoni pizza.

SERVER   Pork chops? Maybe a taco?

CUSTOMER   I thought this was a pizza place.

SERVER   It is, but our specialty is variety.

CUSTOMER   I don't want variety. I just want a
                pizza!

SERVER   Oh.

ANNOUNCER   When you want a pizza--and nothing
                else will do--come to Romano's Pizza.
                We only do what we do best.

BLU'S SHOE STORES

CLERK   I checked in the back and we don't
                have that shoe in your size. But I'm
                sure this one'll fit.

CUSTOMER   That's not the style I wanted.

CLERK   Well, we're out of that exact style,
                but this one's just like it.

CUSTOMER	No, it's not. It's not even the color I wanted.
CLERK	Red, blue--what's the difference? Here, try it on.
CUSTOMER	I can't ... get my foot in.
CLERK	Push! Again! Harder!
CUSTOMER	Ouch!!!
CLERK	There you go. Look at that fit!
CUSTOMER	It's squashing my toes!
CLERK	Snug. Just the way it should be.
CUSTOMER	Take it off! It's killing me!
CLERK	You're just not used to high fashion.
CUSTOMER	I didn't want "high fashion" in the first place!
CLERK	Well, make up your mind. Do you want style or do you want comfort?
ANNOUNCER	If you want style and comfort, come to Blu's--where the shoe fits you.
CUSTOMER	It's not coming off!
CLERK	Pull harder!
CUSTOMER	My toes! I can't feel my toes!

BUD MULLIN'S CANDY BARS

INTERVIEWER   Hello. Today we're coming to you straight from the zoo, where I'm talking with Ollie the Owl.

OLLIE   I take it this is your standard P.R. interview: the usual questions about food, lodgings, and so forth to impress the general public?

INTERVIEWER   That's right, Ollie. Just like last year.

OLLIE   Not just like last year.

INTERVIEWER   What do you mean?

OLLIE   Last year I did thirty minutes on "How I Love Living in the Zoo" and I never saw a single dime.

INTERVIEWER   Ollie, no one gets paid for doing these spots.

OLLIE   Was I good last year?

INTERVIEWER   You were the best.

OLLIE   And you want me to do your show again?

INTERVIEWER   Absolutely.

OLLIE   Then sign here.

INTERVIEWER   What's that?

OLLIE   My contract. It says I get paid in Bud Mullin's Candy Bars.

INTERVIEWER   Candy bars? But you're an owl!

OLLIE   An owl who got wise to the delicious, rich milk chocolate in Bud Mullin's Candy Bars. Do we have a deal or don't we?

INTERVIEWER   Ollie, I ....

OLLIE   No candy--no talkee!

INTERVIEWER   You win, Ollie.

OLLIE   My agent said I would.

                  CURRY'S DEPARTMENT STORE

SPEAKER #1   I like your coat!

SPEAKER #2   Thanks.

SPEAKER #1   If I didn't know better, I'd say it was new.

SPEAKER #2   It is new.

SPEAKER #1   No!

SPEAKER #2   Yes!

SPEAKER #1   But you bought a new coat last year.

SPEAKER #2   I buy a new coat every year.

SPEAKER #1   Wait a minute. I know how much you make. How can you afford it?

SPEAKER #2   I shop smart. I shop at Curry's.

ANNOUNCER   Curry's: Quality and style at affordable prices.

                    WAGNER'S DOG FOOD

KID #1   My dog Pepper is the very best dog
                    in the whole wide world.

KID #2   Uh-uh. My dog's the best.

KID #1   He is not!

KID #2   Is, too!

KID #1   Pepper's more happier than your dog.

KID #2   He is not!

KID #1   Is so!

KID #2   Oh, yeah? How come?

KID #1   'Cause I feed him Wagner's Dry Dog
                    Food.

KID #2   Yeccch!

KID #1   That's not what Pepper says.

ANNOUNCER   Wagner's Dry Dog Food--for the "very
                    best dogs in the whole wide world."

                    BARBARA'S CHOCOLATE CHIP COOKIES

DAD   (FROM OFF) Davey?

DAVEY   Uh oh –

DAD   (FROM OFF) Where are you?

DAVEY   I'm ... in the kitchen, Dad.

DAD   (FROM OFF) What are you doing in
                   there?

DAVEY   Nothing!

DAD   (FROM OFF) Are you eating cookies
                   again?

DAVEY   Me?

DAD   (FROM OFF) Are you?

DAVEY   Nope! Uh-uh! No way!

DAD   (FROM OFF) Honest?

DAVEY   No.

DAD   (FROM OFF) When I tell your mother
                   what you've been up to ...!

DAVEY   But Dad, these are Barbara's
                   Chocolate Chip Cookies!

DAD   (FROM OFF) Barbara's Chocolate Chip
                   Cookies? Uh, Davey, you'd better
                   bring those cookies in here. I'll
                   keep them under surveillance.

DAVEY   What does "under surveillance" mean?

DAD   (FROM OFF) It means, "I won't tell
                   your Mother what you've been up to
                   if you bring me those Barbara's
                   Chocolate Chip Cookies!"

TUCKER'S LONG DISTANCE DIALING

DAUGHTER   Mom, can I call Freddie?

MOTHER   Is he the one who calls you collect?

DAUGHTER   No, that's Tommy.

MOTHER   I thought he was the one who wines
                and dines you--Dutch treat.

DAUGHTER   No, that's Bobby.

MOTHER   Isn't he the one who brings you his
                dirty laundry?

DAUGHTER   No, that's Richie.

MOTHER   I give up. Who's Freddie?

DAUGHTER   He's the one you like.

MOTHER   Oh, that Freddie! Well, by all means,
                call him.

DAUGHTER   Thanks, Mom. I'll tell him you miss
                him.

MOTHER   Miss him?

DAUGHTER   (MOVING OFF) Freddie just moved to
                New York last week.

ANNOUNCER   Thank goodness for Tucker's Long
                Distance Dialing--and for all the
                Freddies in your life, wherever they
                may be!

EXERCISES:

Read over the tags at the end of this chapter.

Go through magazine ads and listen to radio and television commercials to choose tags you would like to work on—ones that feel like something the "natural you" would say. Practice delivering the tags as if each one contained the most important information about the very best product there is.

Now go back and get those tags that you passed up in the first exercise.

Run through your list of characters and let each one record different tags. In playback, decide which character works saying which tag.

Keep notes on this; later you may wish to include a string of tags on your demo CD. We highly recommend that you do so; it is an excellent, quick way of showcasing your talent.

This exercise is designed for doubles, but it can also work for singles.

It involves improvisation and is a terrific way for the non-actor to practice acting.

On individual slips of paper, write one or two lines to describe different people in different situations, then fold the papers and put them into a bowl or a box. Take turns drawing the slips one by one, become those characters, and act out the situations described.

Here's an example: A man and wife, married for a long time, go shopping for a car they've wanted to buy for six months. Notice we did not put in a lot of details; always give just enough information so that you and your partner can make some choices and start a dialogue.

Once you have done a particular situation, put it back in the container. The next time you draw it, do it another way.

TAGS

Silhouettes by Joseph Bean. A cut above the rest.

Nadale's Nifty Neckware. Tie one on.

Who's calling? Andy's Message Service can answer that one.

Hamilton's Hardware. Always the best or you can nail us on it.

Ken's Opera Glasses. They're worth a look.

Dixie's Heavenly Donuts. What a holy experience!

Steven's Underwear. Never leaves you in a bind.

Zubler's Zinfandel. When the occasion is so special, the wine must match it.

Nye's Plant Care. Offers all sorts of growth opportunities.

Burnham's Books for Children. Tall tales for little people.

Cavanaugh's Bakery. Where you can have your cake and eat it, too.

Poole's Party Favors. For all your guests of honor.

Momma and Poppa B's Bingo Parlor. Are you game?

Etherton's Remodeling Service. We'll make your dream home come true.

Songé's Typing Service. The keys to success.

Attention: Funny People! Bulen's Agency for Comedians. We'll put your career on the right laugh track.

Carver's Casino. Fun? You can bet on it!

6.

ANIMATION

THE MANY VOICES IN YOU

ALTHOUGH THERE ARE MANY similarities in the techniques used to attain excellence in both commercial and animation work, the latter really warrants a study all its own. Susan, a veteran animation performer, who now casts and directs animated series, will introduce you to the world of animation and give you a taste of what's involved in creating cartoon voices.

If commercial voice-overs required you to shed a few inhibitions and do a moderate stretch to become a Reassuring Attorney or a Concerned Shopper, now you must really reach to become a Shy Unicorn or a Wicked Monster. Molly Ann says: "We know all about jitters; believe me, we've had them! But if you do manage to shed all remaining inhibitions and take the plunge into this fantastically creative and thrilling world, you won't regret it and you won't ever look back."

The most important thing to remember in discovering all those people who live inside you is to give yourself permission TO PLAY.

When Susan was in school, she used to hide behind her characters. They spoke so she didn't have to, and she made many a trip to the principal's office for trying to impersonate someone in her class. What was then forbidden and punished is now a rewarding profession and a lucrative way of life.

"To find cartoon voices," Susan says, "is to leave your Adult outside the door and find that uninhibited Child inside you. And you won't get kicked out of class for doing it either! Too bad we didn't realize we weren't 'bad' back then—our inhibitions might not be as strong as they are now."

This is probably not the first time you have created a character. You did it with consummate ease and grace when you were a child. When you spoke the words of the Beautiful Princess or the Super Hero, you absolutely believed you were those characters, and so you became them. You worked instinctively, from the inside out, starting with your belief in the existence of the character and then adding a voice, body language, attitudes, and sometimes even a costume and props to go with it. The result? A dynamic, fully developed character was born.

As an adult, you may also have created characters, particularly if you ever read to a child. Can you honestly say you didn't play all the parts in the story? You couldn't help but make the Dragon sound big and threatening, or maybe cute and klutzy and kind. Your Baby Rabbit was little and scared, or laughing and excited—all for the benefit of those wide, wondering eyes and those eager ears that were hanging on your every word. Perhaps you worked in children's theater and brought characters to life by interpreting them with all the belief and drama that were in the colors of the costume you wore. Maybe you just swapped secrets with a special friend at camp many years ago, or told scary ghost stories at slumber parties after football games.

In whatever tales you told or acted out over the years, the voices you used animated the stories. You shared characters that were a part of you, and that fond memory, recent or past, has inspired you now to do cartoons. The techniques we'll discuss will help you re-learn what you knew how to do instinctively as a child.

Where to begin? First, pick a safe and quiet workplace where you won't be interrupted and then . . . giggle. Good. Now giggle some more. Let that giggle grow bigger and bigger until it bursts out of you in a hearty belly laugh. Feels great, doesn't it?

Now fill your mind with ghouls and goblins, and listen to the ghost laugh that comes out of you. Go directly into the vocal sound of this laugh, saying: *Halloween is coming and I'm going to scare everybody who crosses my path!* There—you just animated your voice! You created a character, a Something-That-Goes-Bump-in-the-Night, from a simple laugh.

There are all sorts of ways to come up with cartoon voices, and we will cover many of them in this introductory chapter. Notice you did not change your voice by simply "changing your voice." Instead, you changed your voice by changing what was going on inside you. The amateur's mistake is to find a voice for the character rather than finding the character itself. As with commercial voice-overs, you must become the character. The voice can't help but follow.

Suppose you want to play a little elf. Visualize the elf you want to be. Let's say it is a little boy elf. You don't want him to sound old, but don't just think of him as "young." See him at a particular age. Five? Nine? Twelve? You have the freedom and the fun of choosing. Now suppose you know that this elf boy has a rough-and-tumble attitude, but you want him to be even more aggressive. Just picture him being the toughest elf in the forest—the one with all the wood chips on his shoulder—and he'll automatically sound like a real heavy. Want him to sound nasal? Give him a head cold and feel the congestion. Want him to sound a little silly? Give him an overbite.

Visualization is the key to creating characters. Learn everything you can about the personality and the physicality of the person you are becoming. Delve into the heart and soul of the character and you will organically create its voice. Amateurs speak from the neck up. Excellent voice-over actors speak from the hearts and souls of the characters they know so intimately.

While visualization is essential for achieving excellence in voice-over animation, it may be enhanced by using certain other techniques, such as placement. When we speak in a normal voice, we are in the mid-range of our vocal instrument. When we become nervous or upset, our voice has a tendency to rise in pitch. On a blissfully stress-free day or after a thoroughly relaxing massage, the voice is usually lower and deeper. We can manipulate different placements ourselves to ensure the characters we create continue speaking in their wonderful voices.

There are ten standard vocal placements. Practice each one carefully and see how comfortable you can become with each one before moving on to the next. As with the other exercises in this book, take your time and don't overdo it or you'll wind up with a sore throat. Your vocal chords are muscles; treat them like you would any other muscle in your body. Just as you wouldn't run a 10K race cold without building up your leg muscles, don't force your vocal chords beyond their limits. Let them build slowly and surely, as you build a solid foundation for your talent.

1. The head voice.

Men, try impersonating a female, like Robin Williams in the movie *Mrs. Doubtfire*. Ladies, think of doing Julia Child. Let that voice fill your head and rattle around in there until it knows it's found a home.

2. The eyes.

Here are Susan's tips for this placement: "I always think of Hayley Mills in the movie *Pollyanna*. She had a very youthful sound that was airy, up, and innocent. Also, try thinking of sunshine coming through your eyes. It feels quite bright and British. Think of Kate Winslett in the movie *Titanic*."

3. Nasal.

Speak very frontally right through your nose. Pinch your nostrils with your fingers and say "hello," then let go and try to duplicate that nasal sound. You will probably sound like you have a bad cold—and this is good.

4. Adenoidal.

This is the sound of a bad cold having a bad day. You are the most plugged up you will ever be. Located far back in the nasal cavity, this voice sounds as if your entire head is filled with tissue paper.

5. Near the ears.

Remember the Munchkins in *The Wizard of Oz*? Imitate them now by singing: *Oh, we're off to see the Wizard, the wonderful Wizard of Oz*. Can you feel your ears vibrate? That delightful bubbly sound coming out of you is very cartoony, but extremely lovable.

6. Lower mouth.

Recapture that plugged-up adenoidal feeling, but bring the voice down into the mouth for a mushy sound. Make sure your cheeks are loose and your jaw is flexible. This particular placement has been used for all sorts of cute characters. The "Muttley" Don Messick created for Hanna-Barbera immediately comes to mind.

7. The throat.

Drop your voice into your throat and growl. Very good. Now growl the growl of an Evil Ruler on the brink of losing his kingdom and say: "No one will ever take my kingdom from me—no one!" And *voilà!*— you have created a terrific Villain.

8. Back of the throat.

Move your voice toward the back of your throat and say the word "hello." It should sound like Pee Wee Herman or Kermit the Frog, and is a great voice for nerds, little animals, and even certain thugs.

9. Chest.

Place your voice squarely in your chest and try the word "hello." Did that solid, upright greeting surprise you? It's a natural for honest and sincere heroes and heroines.

10. The diaphragm.

This placement will give you your deepest and strongest voice. It is the sound of power and authority, and it speaks convincingly as either Good or Evil.

BEAU WEAVER

Character voices other than the ones we've described will come to you as you practice these exercises, but remember: The voice is only a small part of the total character. A cute or interesting voice does not make a great cartoon character. You must develop the complete character by visualizing its totality because your job is to make it jump off the page and bring it to life.

Susan, who has directed a number of cartoon shows, has this to say: "Many times when I've been casting, the actor will ask me what I'm looking for. Much of the time we don't know. We may have a good understanding of the character's personality, but often we don't have a specific sound in mind. If you are the one who brings that character to life, we will know it when we hear it."

And speaking of hearing it, how many things don't we hear in the course of an ordinary day? We don't really listen to the blender as it whips up our favorite protein drink. We cringe and block out the motorcycle that roars down our streets. We hurry to slap the ringing alarm clock into silence. We live in a vacuum of sound. But the sounds of the inanimate objects around us are great for helping us find cartoon characters.

Consider the blender. Imitate its whirring, then layer-in words to that sound. Perhaps you came up with the voice of a big, buzzing insect. Maybe you found a different character. As long the character you discovered is interesting and believable, it's worth keeping. Listen to the world around you. Imitate its many sounds and let your imagination run wild and free in discovering more characters.

Animal sounds can also help you come up with many unique and vivid characters to add to your growing repertoire. (Visualization, of course, will flesh them out.) Take the sound of a lamb. That *baaaaa* is a great way to produce the voice of an old man or old lady. Try it now. It might also give you a nervous, insecure character. Work with a variety of animal sounds to explore characters that could speak with those voices.

Another way to find characters is through celebrity impersonations. Here's Susan's success story using this technique: "There was a show that Marvel was doing called *Moondreamers*. After they had seen every guy in town, they got the idea to audition some women. I was one of those women. The character they described to me was very much like a soldier. He wore a little helmet and he spoke with great authority. I felt he might be similar to George C. Scott's portrayal in *Patton*, but I knew if I told the casting director I wanted to do George C. Scott, I would have been laughed out of the studio. So I just did it. I gave them my version of Scott's Patton, with a heart, a soul, and a personality. I had such a clear image of who the character was, I created a complete cartoon entity. And I got the job."

Now you've been cast in an animated show. Congratulations! Know that when you go in to play the part for which you've been cast, you may also be asked to do another role. Animation is a multi-voice business. You may wind up doing as many as three different voices. You'll receive one fee for the first two and an additional ten percent for the third voice. Everybody generally makes the same rate whether they do five lines or fifty.

You may work only one and one-half hours, but you are required to be available for four hours under SAG rules. You will make about a thousand dollars for each episode in which you have performed one or more voices.

This is also a very fast business. While it takes one week to do a twenty-two-minute on-camera sitcom, you will record a twenty-two-minute animation show in four hours or less. As Molly Ann puts it: "When time is so important, you can't be average and you can't be erratic; you must be consistently excellent to make it in voice-overs—commercial or animation."

The following is a list of characters we recommend you develop, and we recommend you develop two voices for each character. Why? After you have been booked to do a guest spot and you are in the studio with other actors preparing to record, you may hear another performer speak in a voice similar to the one you were planning on using. You must be able to come up with another voice ON THE SPOT. If you know your characters inside and out, this won't be a problem.

Hero/Heroine	Nanny
Villain/Villainess	Nurse
Little Furry Animal	Pirate
Butler	Sea Captain
Elf	Gun Moll
Gremlin	Irish Policeman

Remember the laugh exercise we did at the beginning of this chapter? Do it now for all these characters. Remember to picture each character you're working on. Record the exercise and then listen to hear whether each character has a laugh all its own. Once the characters' laughs are distinct and can be summoned up quickly and easily, start speaking in their different voices.

Borrow children's books from the library and read them aloud. Record your efforts and listen to them. Do you believe those characters really exist? Leave messages on your answering machine in different voices. While driving in your car, make up situations for your characters and let them speak the appropriate dialogue. Susan watches old movies on TV and then re-creates the characters' voices. "I try to climb inside each interesting character," she says. "Actually, I get to know them, feel what they're feeling, and the voices just come."

Both animation and commercial voice-overs require you to bring a character to life. But when you walk into that lonely (probably cold and intimidating) booth, your nerves and your surroundings may conspire to do you in. Here's where your imagination and visualization skills can help you succeed.

First of all, pretend that you are not in the booth. Let the setting of the story be your setting. If the tale is one of knights and dragons, let the booth be the castle you're defending from the raging beast. Or let it be the clearing in the forest where you'll fry that nasty old knight with one blast of your flaming breath. If the story is about fairies granting wishes, let the booth be your magic dreamland of marvelous wishes come true.

See the colors of the scenery you've chosen and add as many wonderful details as you can to set the stage for the arrival of your characters. Give them a special place in which to be, then bring them to life by creating their hearts and souls. Don't just "do" voices. Lots of people can do voices; only the best can come up with three-dimensional characters.

For an example of some of the finest animated voice work, watch old Warner Bros.' *Looney Toons* and listen to the brilliant talent of the late Mel Blanc doing his famous Bugs Bunny, Porky the Pig, Daffy Duck, Sylvester, and various other characters. Notice that the voice placements for his characters are quite similar, but the distinct personalities he gave each one created unique, unmistakable individuals that we immediately recognize.

Bugs Bunny is very cocky and self-assured. We believe that he believes he can get himself out of every tough situation. Porky is shy, adorable, and insecure. Mel even gave him a stutter to finesse the character. Sylvester has a frontal lisp and Daffy has a lateral one—further refinements on already well-established characters.

Mel's creations came out of his personality and heart, so they in turn had unique and believable identities. The industry and the world miss this great man, but his very real and vivid characters live on and on.

Is there a place in the world of animation voice-overs for you? There most certainly is—if you are willing to work hard to master the techniques we've described in this chapter and in this book. Perseverance will get you in the door; your talent and your training will allow you to stay there. And you can't just be good—you must be excellent.

Some additional thoughts from Susan: "When I directed *James Bond, Jr.*, I must have seen more than two hundred actors for six different roles.

The competition is fierce, but we are always looking for fresh, new talent. I used several actors that season who were brand new to this art form, but they all had several things in common. Each had a repertoire of characters ranging from heroes to villains to butlers to maids. Many different characters in all shapes and sizes were just straining to come out of the actors and find a place on a show. The actors had been finding and developing all these people who lived inside them for such a long time, and now they were ready to introduce them to the world of animation. There is nothing more exciting than discovering new talent brimming over with full-blown and complete characters."

Voices came easy to us as children. We knew we were the Cowboy, so we could say with absolute conviction, "This town just ain't big enough for the two of us." We believed all those characters we portrayed. We were those characters, so their voices were true. The years passed and, sadly, "growing up" silenced our many voices. Fortunately, animation voice-overs allow us to recapture that spirit—that uninhibited, creative spark that illuminated our childhood worlds—and populate this larger, often lonely, adult world with an abundance of gifts from our hearts and souls.

The following are excerpts from the animation demo scripts of Jan Rabson, Kevin Schon, and Mona Marshall. These wonderfully talented voice-over artists have generously agreed to let us share this material with you.

```
                    ADVENTURES IN SPACE
                    by Mona Marshall


(1940s PIANO)


ANNOUNCER          Good evening, Ladies and Gentlemen,
                   and welcome to Mellow Drama's Live
                   Radio Theatre, brought to you tonight
                   from the terribly chic, too, too
                   sleek and cheeky, posh and peaky,
                   Sportmen's Lodge Lounge, where the
                   high, low and in-between mingle
                   amidst the tingle of almost crystal
                   (at least it's glass, not plastic),
                   and the conversation ranges from the
                   audaciously austere to the morbidly
                   mundane. Please note: Unlike the
```

name suggests, there are no animal
heads adorning the walls, perhaps
the tables from time to time on a
particularly raucous evening ... but
not the walls. Instead we have our
own sweet sight of serenity: Sam, the
supple and sagacious swan. (POINT TO
SAM). But enough about ambiance and
atmosphere and on with our show.

ANNOUNCER   Tonight, we bring you a story
of subtle strength, (STING) of
super-human struggle, (STING)
of science-fiction supremacy.
(STING) A saga so superior
in its scope, so sublime in
its summation, that it stuns
the senses. Tonight, Ladies
and Gentlemen, we bring you
(BIG ROLL) Sheldon and Sheila
Soloman's sensational bestselling short story, now a radio
serial.

ADVENTURES IN
SPACE (ORGAN
THEME)   But, first a word from our sponsor.
("NBC CHIME")

(SWEET FLOWING
MUSIC)

COMMERCIAL   Hello. Is your love life less than
lustful? Is your lover's libido
lacking or lost? Is your heart
hungering for a handsome hunk that
isn't hamburger? ... If that's the
problem, your solution is to give him
everything you are ... NOTHING. (STOP
MUSIC) Yes. Wear NOTHING and he'll be
eating out of your ... hand. (NOTHING
STING)

ANNOUNCER   And now ... ADVENTURES IN ... SPACE ... (ORGAN THEME)

(HEROIC MUSIC)

NARRATOR   It is the year 2090 A.D. A group of intergalactic youngsters and their teachers are traveling in their vehicular space module, heading toward the moon on a routine lunar expedition, when suddenly and inexplicably their flight pattern is altered and they are forced to land on a hitherto unknown planet. (ROCKET CRASH)

(EERIE SPACE MUSIC)

TOMMY   Wow, look at this place. Hey, this might even be more exciting than an old moon expedition.

KENJI   Ah, Tommy-san, is this cool or what? We don't even need "Wet" suits.

MOGO   Yo, homeboy Kenji, that's weight suit!

KENJI   That's what I said, "Weight suit."

MOGO   In that case you said it right. This here's badder than a lunar flight.

ALEXANDER   I don't know if that is a valid evaluation of our situation, MoGo. According to my calculations we are approximately 1,729 kilometers past the fifteenth triad parallel, which I deduce to mean that ...

BENJY   Whoa ... We could be in big, big trouble. I don't know, you guys. It looks kinda scary to me. Those are

weird-looking trees. The branches
look like giant bony fingers that
could reach out and grab us.

MEG   Don't worry, Benjy. Do remember, we're
                     all Junior Explorers. We'll simply
                     look at this as another deliriously
                     delicious deviation from the doldrums.

MICHAEL   That's right, Meg, the only thing we
                     have to worry about is ... Where in
                     the Universe are we? (STING)

SUZANNA   Oh, Michael, you have to be just about
                     the finest specimen of young manhood
                     I've ever seen. Cross my heart and
                     hope to have hushpuppies ... Oooo, you
                     are magnificent! I do hope there's a
                     quiet place for us to be alone.

VAL   Oooo, yeah, Mikey Babes, you are
                     definitely a TRD, as in Totally Rad
                     Dude. Oooo, this place is really
                     weird. I wonder if they have a
                     shopping mall and if they do, if
                     they'll take credit cards.

SURFLEY   Whoa, Val, good point! I wonder if
                     they've some gnarly waves here, too.
                     Bitchin'! (MUSIC OUT)

MAJOR GERMACK   All right, you little Rocket Rats,
                     quickly gather 'round the space
                     vehicle ... the captain has something
                     she wants to tell you.

CAPTAIN   Junior Explorers, due to a technical
                     snafu beyond our control, we've had
                     to make an unscheduled landing on
                     what looks to be in my estimation
                     some ... tough turf. So while we
                     adults explore the area, you children
                     are to stay here with the spacecraft.

CHILDREN	Aw, aw, aw, aw, aw, aw, Bummer.
LT. CHEKOV	Calm yourselves, my little Comrades, there is much work to do here. We will leave Kiko the Computer and Miko the Mutant Maltese to help you.
KIKO	Thank you, Lt. Chekov, your verbal expression of confidence is appreciated and has been filed under compliment.
MIKO	(Gurgle-growl) Compliment nice, but Miko want a cookie.
MARGARET	Here, Miko, we can share.
MIKO	(Gobble) All gone. Miko no like to share. Miko need walk.
MARGARET	Okay, as soon as the adults leave I'll take you for a walk over by that dark, scary cave ... maybe we can find some Monsters! (Giggle)
MIKO	No way, what are you? Nuts!
(NEW EERIE MUSIC)	
NARRATOR	And, as we leave our seemingly secure and serene scene of space survivors, we see that some unsavory subhuman species have been spying on our unsuspecting subjects. (STING)
EVIL 1	Oh, look, looky, looky there ...
EVIL 2	Oh, yes, Mistress, your prestigious plot is working precisely as you planned.
EVIL 3	Oh, yes, oh, yes, oh, yes ... the

adults are leaving the children unguarded ... Goody, goody, goody!

MISTRESS   Ooooohhhm shut up, you Slobbering Simpletons, those brats are not unguarded, they have their radically advanced K12 KO Z Computer and their stupidly affectionate pet Mutant Maltese to protect them! Oh, Dratted Sunshine and Lightness, how I hate those sickeningly loveable beasts with their insatiable appetites for sweets!

EVIL PET   Mistress is right. The computer can sense us and warn them of our presence and their beast could pierce through our hearts, and kill us with kindness ... and calories. (STING)

ALL EVIL   Ah, ah, ah, ah, ah ...

MISTRESS   Ahhhh, we must get them before they discover us and uncover ... THE SECRET!

NARRATOR   And what, you may ask sitting there in your comfortable chair, is the dark and nefarious secret these mysterious minions of evil embrace so closely to their breasts? And will they adopt any arduous implements of terrifying torture to subdue the spirit, not to mention the bodies, of our spunky space survivors?

ANNOUNCER   For the answer to these questions, and many more, tune in again next week for: ADVENTURES IN SPACE ... (SPACE THEME) Until then, good night and good musing.

PART TWO

ANNOUNCER   Good evening, Ladies and Gentlemen,
                 and welcome to Part 2 of ADVENTURES
                 IN SPACE.

NARRATOR   When last we left our spunky space
                 survivors, they were about to be
                 detrimentally deterred by those
                 malevolent minions of maliciousness.
                 But fear not, no, indeed, you see,
                 more sociable, solicitous species
                 have been spying on the spies.

GOOD 1   Oh my, it looks like those poor
                 children may need our help.

GOOD 2   Oh my dear, you're absolutely right.

GOOD 3   Yes, we're talking major evil here.
                 The kind of dire diehard decadence
                 and deceit we are dedicated to
                 destroy and defeat with due diligence
                 ... in other words ... no dallying
                 ... those darlings are in desperate
                 despair ... They could get dumped on!

GOOD 4   Yeah, let's savage the suckers!

NARRATOR   So will those gritty, gallant Good
                 Gals indeed savage the suckers? Or
                 will the sweet unsuspecting space
                 survivors escape the unsavory sub-
                 human species that would subject
                 them to a fate worse than swallowing
                 slimy, salty salamanders?

ANNOUNCER   Tune in again next week at the same
                 time to find out the answer to
                 that question and many more as we
                 bring you the next episode of ...
                 ADVENTURES IN SPACE ...

                 Good night and good musing.

AUDITION SCRIPT
by Kevin Schon

STEVE (Handsome jock, 17 years old)	Hi, Wendy! Gosh, uh, you look really terrific tonight! Uh, what I mean is ... You always look terrific! Hey, we better get going. We're gonna miss the kickoff!
PROFESSOR STUBBINS (Kindly wizard, 66 years old)	Oooh, I've forgotten the spell again ... Uh, let's see ... Three F's ... Uh ... Fee ... Fi ... Fo ... Oh, no, that's not it ... Uh ... Full fathom five ... My father ... No, no, no! Uh ... Eh ... Fee ... Uh ... Fi ... Uh ... Fo ... Ooooh Fiddlesticks!
WHIMSY (Mischievous elf)	(Giggle) Silly! Why, this isn't just any old forest ... This is a magic forest! Anything can happen here!
MR. SPINGE (Seductive villain)	Why, hello, my dear ... What's a nice ... plump ... tasty-looking little thing like you doing in the middle of the deep, dark forest? Aren't you afraid to be out here all by yourself?
BUDDY (Dopey little bear)	Oh, boy ... Somebody ate the blueberry bundt cake I baked for Billy Beasley's birthday. Oh, now what am I going to do?
MARVIN (Frantic nerd)	Can I come with you, Professor? Huh, can I, huh, huh? I won't get in the way. I won't touch anything this time, I promise. Oh, please, say yes, say yes, say yes, say yes, PLEASE say yes!
ERNIE (Rowdy, rough and tough cowpoke)	Howdy, mah name is Ernie and I'm a cowboy hairdresser! Yep, that's right. Cowboys like to look good,

too! `Course, they don't like it to get around, so keep it under your hat!

MAYOR BOFF (Pompous blowhard)	My fellow limptoads! Today is a day that will live forever in limptoad history! Uh ... yes. That is, eh ... hysterically, I mean, HISTORICALLY speaking. I'm talking about ... eh ... what am I talking about?
LITTLE BOO (Adorable 8-year-old)	Oh, gee, I don't think we should go in there. It looks awfully dark and spooky. And what's that awful smell? Oh! I think I hear my mom calling me. I have to go home now! Bye!
BELDAR (Hero--a bit too full of himself)	Don't despair, Princess! I will lead you through the labyrinth and return you safely to Gaffonia. Put your arms around my neck and hold on tightly. (Choking) Not ... quite ... that ... tightly ...
NICK (Tough Bronx Italian, 35 years old)	Hey, how you doin'? Yer listenin' ta Nick, on W.A.R.T., yer arts and classics station. Comin' up next ... Da first movement of *Cosi Fan Tutti*. So ... get yer fan tutti cozy, and we'll be right back.
WINKY (Snooty scientist)	Obviously you don't have the slightest idea what I'm talking about. (Sigh) Very welllll ... Pay attention and I'll see if I can't explain this in a way that even YOU can understand.
BRATLEY (Snotty little brat)	Oh wait, wait, don't tell me, I know. The numerator is on the top and the denominator is on the bottom, huh? Whaddya ya mean that's not right? OK, fine, the denominator is on the top

and the numerator is on the bottom.
Ahhh, who cares anyway?!

O'HAVER (Big,   Hah, hah, hah, hah, hah, hah! Dat'll
dumb jerk of a   teach ya' to get outta da way, punk!
dog)   Ha, ha, ha, ha, ha! Awwwww ... Did
                 he hurt his widdle paw? What a dweeb!
                 What a doofus! What a weenie dawg!
                 Ha, ha, ha, ha!

GRAMPS (Grumpy   Would you just look at this mess!
old man)   Those little blue bozos have really
                 done it this time! That does it! I'm
                 gonna get my fly swatter and go pay
                 those little pip-squeaks a visit!

AUNTIE ETHEL   (Sings) "I'm in the mood for looove
(Wacky witch,   ... Simply because you're near me ...
always lookin'   and every time you're near me, I'm in
for love)   the mood for love." Come on honey,
                 let's smooch! Kiss me, you fool, or
                 I'll turn you into a slug!

HANNA-BARBERA AUDITION
by Jan Rabson

ROD SERLING   Witness if you will, a world of
                   animation. A new dimension of sight
                   and sound. You are about to enter
                   a different realm where reality and
                   fantasy take on new aspects. There's
                   a signpost up ahead - Jan Rabson
                   doing a 3-to-5-minute voice-over
                   audition at Hanna-Barbera Zone.

NARRATOR   Once upon a time ...

NERD   Hey, this sounds like a fairy tale.

NARRATOR   Not quite ... in a land far away
                   known as Larynxland, there lived a
                   king named ...

NERD   Tonsillectomy (Laugh)

NARRATOR   Who, pray tell, are you?

NERD   Oh, hi, I'm Nerd Guard Jr. and I
                   go to Northridge College to study
                   accounting so I can be like my
                   father, well, not really, because I
                   want to own my own firm, see, and
                   he works for, like, a small little
                   company, although he has his own
                   secretary, which is pretty cool ...

NARRATOR   Are you quite through?

NERD   I think so.

NARRATOR   Every year there was a ...

TEENAGER   It's my turn. Every year there an
                   Ugliest Man in the Kingdom contest.
                   The winner got 10,000 dulmas--that's

                      about 160 dollars. All the ugly men
                      lined up and the king judged the
                      winner.

OLD BRIT   Why, there they are, ugly brutes.
                      Reminds me of the time I was in
                      New Guinea--or was it Rhodesia? The
                      natives were rather restless--or were
                      they on the warpath? No matter, there
                      was tension in the air--or was it
                      something else--maybe it was a small
                      fever going about.

GOOD OL' BOY   Wow, you've been just about
                      everywhere and done everything. This
                      is my first time watching one of
                      these ugly contests. I'll bet you've
                      seen a bunch, huh?

TERRY THOMAS   If I recall correctly, last year's
                      contest was quite exciting. The
                      gentleman, and I use the term ever
                      so loosely, was so ugly when he took
                      off his hat that they arrested him
                      for carrying a concealed weapon.

EMCEE   And without any further ado, I
                      present to you the man who gave you
                      taxation without representation,
                      a mere figurehead, a bumbling,
                      inefficient monarch, an anachronism
                      and a blight on the human race--your
                      king.

THE KING   Oh, thank you, thank you. A very
                      nice speech indeed. Ohhhh, my. Before
                      we begin the contest, are there any
                      questions?

THE PRINCE   Yes. Your highness, could you tell
                      me why every year we debase and
                      humiliate our fellow man in such an
                      infantile and demeaning manner?

THE KING	Who was that young snit?
EMCEE	Your son ... the Prince, sire.
THE KING	Oh, I thought he looked familiar.
EAST INDIAN	If I may be philosophic on the question put forth by this young and quite inquisitive lad, the contest is merely a ... Hey, what are you doing? Put me down ... leave me alone.
JEWISH	Look, the ugly persons are lining up, and so painful to look at. Speaking of pain, this finger hurts me, but this finger doesn't hurt me half as much as this finger hurts me ...
EMCEE	Take your places, please.
BIG DEEP VOICE	I'm really not that ugly. I'm only doing this contest till my big break comes in show business ... actually, I'm a dancer.
FRENCH	The fact is I am not ugly at all. I am extremely handsome. I know this, and this is what makes me ugly. I am so conceited and egotistical that people can't stand to be around me.
MEEK	I'm probably the ugliest person here. I need that prize money. It's been a dream of mine for years to open up a shoe store for hard-to-fit sizes.
BRONX	Hey, hold your horses ...
BIG DEEP VOICE	Was he referring to me?
BRONX	Look what I found. If this ain't the ugliest guy I ever saw, I don't know

what is. I had to put a sack over his head he was so beastly.

GRAVEL VOICE   You lousy, stupid, moronic idiot. I'll see you're hung for this! You'll never know another minute of peace! I'll make your life hell if it's the last thing I do!

BRONX   He even talks ugly. It's perfect.

BROOKLYN   I don't want to bust your bubble or nothing, but I got to tell you that the guy you got there ain't no ugly man, but an ugly woman ... uh, I mean ... that's the Queen!

THE PRINCE   Hey, that's my mom!

BRONX   You're kidding. Oh, I'm really sorry, Your Highness ... I, uh, I didn't recognize you with the beard.

NARRATOR   And so our story ends. The King declared that the Queen was indeed the winner of the contest. The man who found her was awarded 10,000 dulmas. The Queen swore she would never speak to the King again, and the King ... lived happily ever after.

7.

THE DEMO CD

EMOS—A DEMO IS YOUR calling card. It is to voice-over what a picture and résumé are to an on-camera actor. The recording should be all of the best that you are with range and authenticity. Probably the best piece of advice is: DO NOT DO A DEMO UNTIL YOU ARE READY. Wait until you feel you are at the top of your game.

It is very tempting to take a class or two and feel the urge and enthusiasm to hurry up, get a demo, and throw your hat in the ring. However, if you are still climbing up the learning curve and developing your skills, you will want to wait until you have a firm handle on your craft. You must feel confident that you can pick up a piece of copy, any copy, and know how to give a terrific cold reading. If it's for a commercial, the reading should be conversational. As Susan says, "You must take the words off the page; reading while giving the illusion that you are not reading." The same holds true for animation. You must have a firm grasp of how to make your characters real, authentic, and varied. You also must be able to call up your roster of characters at will, or create new ones on the spot.

Once you have your voice-over technique down, you should begin interviewing demo producers. Listen to samples they have produced. Do the spots sound real? Are they "posted" (with background music and sound effects) effectively to support the voice-over, but not overpower it? Is each spot on the demo fully produced? If so, you've found your producer.

What you don't want to hear is a particular theme or signature of the demo producer. The demo should be about you and your talent, not the producer. Each demo should showcase the unique range and talent of the individual artist. Creating a good demo can be costly, but it's an investment an artist must make in order to compete in the marketplace. If done well, that demo can serve you for many years. Fortunately, demos are cheaper to produce than they used to be because we no longer use tapes that require professional duplication or expensive labels and covers. We can now keep expenses down by doing duplication and labeling on our own personal computers.

Paying the very highest price for a demo doesn't necessarily ensure you're getting the best package, but don't look for a bargain, either. A demo that is not professionally produced stands out as much as an excellent one, and that's not good! Get referrals from agents and other actors, then interview and investigate on your own. Find out how much time will be allotted for the recording. You don't want to feel rushed or suffer performance anxiety, which will only have a bad effect on your readings. This can happen when an artist is working at an hourly rate rather than a fixed price for the complete project. The best demo producers consider a demo done when excellence has been achieved and won't send you out the door with anything less than your best.

Generally, demos should average between one and two minutes tops. When you sign with a voice-over agent, you will work together to edit a one-minute version, either by omitting some of the pieces altogether or reducing the length of individual spots.

It is up to you whether you use actual copy or create original material for your demo CD. There are pros and cons to both approaches. In general, it is okay to use real audition copy as long as your use of the material is for talent demonstration purposes only.

If you write your own copy (or have someone else write it for you), you can surprise your listeners with fresh, new material that will hold their interest. However, good copy, while it is easy to recognize, is not always easy to write. Get several independent and objective opinions about the quality of your original material before you put it on your demo. Creating an authentic-sounding ad or spot from a magazine ad is a terrific idea. It gives you the product name, some copy, and all of the fine points that the advertiser is trying to convey. Just change it a little and put it in your own words.

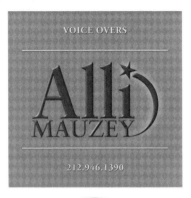

VOICE OVERS

Alli MAUZEY

212.946.1390

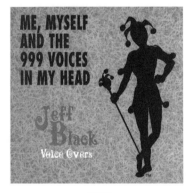

Alli MAUZEY

VOICE OVERS

212.946.1390

Steve Staley

Commercial
Animation

Steve Staley

Commercial
Animation

at&a
arlene thornton & associates.inc.
talent agency

(818) 760-6686
fax (818) 760-1185

12001 ventura place • suite 201 • studio city, ca 91604

ME, MYSELF
AND THE
999 VOICES
IN MY HEAD

Jeff Black

Voice Overs

Jeff Black

1. COMMERCIAL
2. ANIMATION
3. CELEB IMPRESSIONS

John Huey

Voice Over

John Huey
818-848-4666

1. Commercials
2. Animation
3. Narrations

Voice Over

Michael F. Smith

Commercial & Animation VoiceOver Demo

Michael F. Smith

1. Commercial (2:03)
2. Animation (2:24)

(714) 336-7657
MSmith@VoiceOverLA.com
www.VoiceOverLA.com

NATALINA MAGGIO

VOICE OVER
ANIMATION DEMO

NATALINA MAGGIO
ANIMATION DEMO

(818)427-8221
natalina@natalinamaggio.com   www.natalinamaggio.com

HAVE YOU HEARD
PATRICK
PINNEY?

LEND AN EAR

LEND AN EAR

HAVE YOU HEARD
PATRICK
PINNEY?

FOR HIRE   MIGHTY FRESH FLAVOR
Rick Weiss
Naturally Flavored VOICEOVER

FOR HIRE   MIGHTY FRESH FLAVOR
Rick Weiss
Naturally Flavored VOICEOVER

1 COMMERCIAL 2 CHARACTER

VOICES UNLIMITED
(312)832-1113

CYNTHIA TEACHING HER STUDENTS.

SUE TEACHING HER STUDENTS.

Devon Bowman makes us sound good.

Voice-over artists often use a mixture of actual prerecorded material and original copy. We recommend that you use whatever best showcases your talents. As a beginner, do the first spot on your demo CD in your own natural voice. This answers the question agents and casting directors always ask: "What does this person really sound like?" Once they have this point of reference, they are more apt to show interest in discovering your entire range of voices and characters. And remember that on commercial demos it's more about different attitudes than voices. As a matter of fact, you only need your own natural voice with all your personalities.

You must grab your listeners with a dynamite spot within the first ten to fifteen seconds or they will stop listening to your demo and move on to the next. Use commercials that won't date you. If you choose a recognizable spot that is several years old, casting people will wonder how old your entire demo is.

What if you don't have a variety of interesting voices? If you have only one or two characters, but you do them extremely well, don't try to pad your demo with voices that are less than excellent. It is better to do one minute of what you do well—impress your listeners—than to clutter your demo with unsuccessful attempts at variety and lose your appreciative audience.

Vary your spots in terms of pacing, pitch, hard- and soft-sells, long and short copy. Never let your longer pieces run more than twenty seconds.

If you do impressions, make sure they are dead on. If people could hear voice-over artist Frank Welker do Gregory Peck, they would never put down a less-than-perfect impression of him again!

There is disagreement in the industry as to whether or not you should include a double on your demo. Some professionals feel that a double is needed to prove that you can work well with another person. Others are concerned that your listeners may be more impressed with your partner's voice than with your own. If you do opt to include a double, choose a partner of the opposite sex.

As your talent evolves, so should your demo. Jack Angel, a successful voice actor, suggests that once you have a good, recognizable, professional commercial to your credit, you should begin your demo with that spot. New material can easily be cut into your master at any time to replace older spots, or you can record a whole new demo if you prefer.

The demo represents you. In your absence, it auditions for you. Therefore, it should always showcase your very best work and be of the highest quality. When it is heard, you will not be around to plead, "I could have done better if I'd had better copy"; or (our favorite) "The engineer is my brother-in-law, so I had to use him. Actually, he's not really an engineer, but he plans to go to school for it next year."

Once you choose the material for your demo and determine the order in which you want to present it, you need an engineer to select the music and sound effects you want to include. Don't discount the effects of using background music on your demo. In addition to establishing a particular mood, music and sound effects greatly add to the flow and dynamics of your production. It is a distinctive touch that will enhance the professionalism of your demo.

The following are examples of two types of demo scripts. The first one was written for a woman who wanted to showcase her commercial characters. The copy also has a "through-line" or story that runs the length of the script.

The second script was written for a man. He wanted to demonstrate a few of his characters but also include some spokesperson work, as well as tags.

Where individual character names are so personal that they might not identify a particular voice for you, we have simply written in the type of voice we mean. SFX indicates "sound effects" or "music."

MUSIC—ESTABLISH means we should hear a few bars of the specified music—just enough to establish a mood—before the character begins to speak. THEN UNDER means that the music is to continue while the next speaker does his or her spot, then it stops.

SFX	ANIMAL SOUNDS--ESTABLISH, THEN UNDER
WANDA	Hello. Wanda Wonder here at the zoo. Today we're talking with Lyle the Lion.
LYLE	(FEROCIOUS GROWL)
WANDA	The very large lion. How're you doing, Lyle?
LYLE	*Comme çi, comme ça.*

WANDA	Could you be a little more specific?
LYLE	No.
WANDA	Would you like to tell our friends about your life here in the zoo?
LYLE	No.
WANDA	I knew this wouldn't work. Well, moving right along to the monkey cage ... Uh. Lyle? You have your paw on my shoulder.
LYLE	I know.
WANDA	Look, Lyle, I have to go now. I'll call you, okay? We'll do lunch.
LYLE	How about today?
WANDA	What?
LYLE	Lunch. Today.
WANDA	Oh, gee, I'd love to, but I already ...
LYLE	(FEROCIOUS GROWL)
WANDA	Today would be great! I'm starving!
LYLE	You're a real doll, Wanda.
SFX	MUSIC BOX PLAYING--ESTABLISH, THEN UNDER
MOTHER	My daughter Lisa got a new doll for her birthday. She named her Jeannie. Lisa says Jeannie is her very best friend.

TEENAGER   Mother, get real. Lisa's best friend is food. I mean, she practically lives in the refrigerator. I made this pie for Brian--he's this totally outrageous guy my parents can't stand--and Lisa ate the whole thing. She is, like, such a pain.

OLD WOMAN   Pain? You don't know pain until you have dentures. Each morning they go in and by noon they fall out. Usually in public.

SFX   SANDPAPER SCRATCHING UNDER

BROOKLYN ACCENT   Are you bothered by flaky fall-out? Do you ever get the itch for long-lasting relief? Try new Flake-Off for problem dandruff, and scratch that itch for good.

SFX   SEXY MOOD MUSIC UNDER

FRENCH DIALECT   "Good" is not enough when it comes to champagne. The French know it must be the best or it should never touch your lips. And the best champagne is Duval. Duval--*le meilleur champagne du monde.*

WITCH   How about a nice French apple pie, dearie? No? How can I cast a spell if you won't cooperate?

SFX   SAME MUSIC BOX PLAYING--ESTABLISH, THEN UNDER

KID   (CALLING) Mom, how do you spell "broken?" I'm writing this note to thank Uncle Al for my doll Jeannie, and I want to tell him all about her. And Mom? We're all out of pies, cakes, and cookies!

SFX   STING

The next script has no through-line. It is composed of separate, individual spots. Some people prefer using this type of script because they feel their audience's attention will be focused completely on the voices and not on following a story, especially if the copy consists of prerecorded material.

Although we have used fictitious company or product names in the following demo script, the material should give you an idea of what using actual copy would be like.

Also, we have deliberately left out any sound notations this time. As an exercise, try selecting appropriate music and sound effects for this script.

DAD
I'm a freelance writer. For years my kids kept telling me: "Dad, get a computer." And I kept telling them: "Every day I fight with editors and publishers. I don't need to fight a machine, too." That was before my kids bought me a Tangerine computer. Now my work practically writes itself, thanks to my Tangerine computer!

ATTORNEY
When the IRS computer eats your tax refund, call us. When your poodle plows under your neighbor's Victory Garden, call us. When the diamond lasts forever but the marriage doesn't, call us. We're the law offices of Fold, Bend, Staple and Mutilate--and we understand.

COOL DUDE
My lady. Here I am again, waiting for her to put on her makeup. Right about now she's doing her eyes. But what she does to those eyes is sensational! I call it "magic." She says it's X Factor. Magic or X Factor? Maybe the X Factor is the magic. Whatever it is, it's worth waiting for!

OLD MAN   The people at College U. believe that
                   learning never stops--and it never
                   stops being fun, either. At College
                   U. anyone can take an extension
                   class, even me. Especially me--I'm
                   not about to stop having fun!

CONSTRUCTION   Out here nails get driven, pounded.
WORKER   In the course of a day, your nails
                   take a terrible beating, too. But you
                   can fight back with Claw-Care. Put
                   it on before bed. Claw-Care takes
                   the night shift and works straight
                   through so you can wake up to
                   stronger, healthier nails. Claw-Care
                   --helps you build better nails.

TAGS:

Vera's Vegetable Oil--the only way to fry.

Sadie's Swim Wear--it'll suit you ... just fine.

Chevillac--it'll drive you ... wild!

Knot's Shoelaces--they're fit to be tied!

Heaven's Scent--when the pursuit is no longer trivial.

CRUISE DIRECTOR   What's the best way to get from
                   L.A. to L.A.? Board a luxuriously
                   comfortable Dreamboat Cruise ship in
                   L.A. and sail down the coast with
                   us. Shop, sun, and explore the ports
                   of Xihuatanejo, Puerto Vallarta, and
                   Acapulco. Then relax and feast your
                   way back home. Dreamboat Cruises. The
                   best way to get from L.A. to L.A.

IRISH DIALECT   Have you searched the world over for
                   a place you could go? Far away from
                   the bother, with the feelings of
                   home? Come to Ireland this summer,

where you'll find yourself welcome.
Caed mille failtes to Ireland--
welcome to our home.

Once you have recorded your demo, what is the next step?

Make duplicate copies (dupes) to send to agents, casting directors, and ad agencies.

How do you submit a demo?

Simply send it to the appropriate agents, casting directors, and ad agencies. Include a succinct cover letter announcing who you are, (hopefully) who referred you, and necessary contact information so they can reach you.

Where can you find those people?

The Voice-Over Resource Guide is a terrific directory with just about every source a voice-over artist needs—from demos to instruction to representation, etc. They also have an internet site: www.voiceoverresourceguide.com. Actors unions are also a good source: Screen Actors Guild and AFTRA. We have also included a resource guide at the end of this book.

We have included three sample cover letters. These are only starting points. Use your imagination to create your own distinctive attention-grabbers, and remember to keep your letters (like your demo) "short, sweet, and super!"

```
                              Your street address
                              Your city, state, zip

                              The date

Ms. _____, Casting Director
Tremble, Tumble and Thimble Advertising Agency
Their street address
Their city, state, zip

Dear Ms. _____,


Last night I attended the annual school play at my
alma mater, Braintrust College. I noticed in the
program that you directed the show. I thoroughly
enjoyed the production--you did a great job!

I understand that you are also the casting director
for Tremble, Tumble and Thimble. I am a voice-over
artist and would appreciate your taking a moment to
listen to my demo (enclosed).

Thank you for your time and I'm looking forward to
seeing the next play you direct!

                              Sincerely,

                              Your signature
                              Your name, typed
```

Since the format of the following letters remains the same, we have simply included the bodies of the letters. This next one is to an agent.

```
Dear Mr. _____,


Do you know me? Most people don't. That's why I
always carry my demo with me. I never leave home
without it. PLEASE don't leave your office without
listening to it!

                              Sincerely
                              (and I mean that),
```

This next letter is also to an agent, but it is more conservative.

```
Dear Mrs. _____,


I am a voice-over artist and am seeking
representation. I do straight and character voices,
and have enclosed a copy of my demo for your
consideration.


I may be reached by phone at _____ or by e-mail
at _____.


                    Thank you.


                    Sincerely,
```

Our recommendations may sound like a lot of tedious and unnecessary work, but it is this attention to detail that distinguishes the professional from the amateur. Show that you know how to handle all phases of the business—like a professional—and, amazingly enough, that's when people will start treating you like one.

8.

THE AGENT

T IS IMPORTANT TO remember that an agent's roster of voice-over talent consists of more than just one client. If your agent represents twenty voice-over artists (and that's a very conservative number!), he or she can spend only five percent of his/her time promoting you. You, however, can spend one-hundred percent of your time promoting you. Along with developing voice-over excellence, it is your responsibility to do everything you can to promote yourself (see Chapter Nine).

SO WHY BOTHER HAVING AN AGENT?

Because independent producers and casting directors contact agents when they need voice-over talent.

Furthermore, the bulk of the copy that you will read (the audition material) will be at your agency. Typically, most copy for commercials is sent to agents who then call in those actors they represent who are appropriate for the spots. Only those they believe can book the job are asked to come in and audition, or "read in the booth," as it known in the industry. Voice-over agencies are equipped with recording booths, as well as a booth director to record your reads and offer appropriate direction.

Agents post their clients' voice-over demos on Voicebank (www. voicebank.net) to showcase their talent. The demos are approximately one minute in length and are categorized by the agents first according to gender and then in groupings of commercial, animation, promo, and narrative. These one-minute demos are also made available on CDs that the agents can submit to producers, directors, casting directors, and ad agencies to showcase their clients and help them book jobs. Agents will also submit copies of your very own CD in its full form (the longer version) to display your ability for a particular job or simply to make the people who can hire you familiar with you, your talent, and your range. In this way, producers and casting directors who have heard an artist's demo can request that actor for a job or an audition.

One of the most important functions of your agent is to negotiate your job to garner the best rate of pay. Your agent is also responsible for booking your jobs and notifying you of the date, time, and place of your recording.

HOW DO YOU GET AN AGENT?

For the fortunate few who already have an agent for theatrical or on-camera commercial work, that agent may be willing to sign them up for voice-overs. The rest of us play the time-honored game of hide-and-seek to get agents. They hide; you seek.

"GETTING" AN AGENT BEGINS WITH "FINDING" AN AGENT. WHERE DO THOSE ELUSIVE PEOPLE HIDE THEMSELVES?

The Internet is a great place to start. You can use your search engine to find voice-over agents in your area.

Voicebank.net lists agents across the United States and Canada. There are also entertainment directories, such as *The Voice-Over Resource Guide* (which is also available on the web at www.voiceoverresourceguide.com). Also, try the actors' unions: SAG and AFTRA.

Before you start making phone calls, try to find out from another source—your teacher, friends in the business, trade papers, or entertainment-industry directories—whether each agency is large or small. Does it have a separate, long-standing, or recently created voice-over division?

Some actors, such as Jack Angel, recommend that a beginner go with a smaller agency or with a newly established voice-over division within an existing agency. In both cases, the agents may be more likely to be open to screening new talent. They also want to be successful, and discovering excellent new talent (that's you!) makes them look very good indeed. But don't be afraid to contact the larger agencies, too. We know many cases where large agencies take on fresh new talent when they truly believe in them.

Call the agencies you want to approach, ask the receptionist for the name of the person who represents voice-over talent, then ask to speak to that agent. Whether you actually speak to the agent or get bogged down at a more clerical level, be brief and keep your tone courteous, positive, and professional. Identify yourself and state your reason for calling. Ask if you may send in your demo CD. You may be told that the agency is not interested in taking on any more voice-over people at this time. If so, make a note to check back with them in one or two months. Write down the name of the person with whom you spoke—later, when you call back, you can address him or her by name and possibly score a few points.

When you do get the green light and are told to mail in your demo, double-check the complete address and the spelling of the name of the person to whose attention you will be submitting your demo. Agents change agencies and agencies change addresses with a frequency that seems to alarm only people who are outside the business.

Draft a cover letter (see Chapter Seven) and mail in your demo promptly. Then what? Sit back and wait for an answer? Not on your life! Never stop with one agent, who might be very busy and can't get to your demo for months. Always do multiple submissions. You might want to change the color of the cover or the font of the lettering on different mailings so that each will look different and new. This is especially easy to do if you are creating your own labels and covers on your personal computer.

After a reasonable amount of time—about two weeks—you may call to see if your demo arrived and if the agent has had a chance to listen to it. If the agent hasn't yet played your demo, check back in another two weeks. Always remain polite and professional; never demand to know when the agent will get to it.

Agent Arlene Thornton of Arlene Thornton and Associates says, "I don't mind people calling after a reasonable amount of time—two or three weeks—but calling too soon or too often turns me off."

If the agent has listened to your demo, you may be informed that you have been turned down. There can be any number of reasons for the rejection: The agency may have "a conflict," which means they already represent someone who sounds "just like you"; or they need someone with more of a range than you have; or they just found out they are moving (again!) and can't be bothered; or they just "aren't interested."

Whatever the reason, and whether or not you agree with it (or even believe it), do not take it personally. Remain professional and don't argue.

If an agent says no, but takes the time to offer you some constructive criticism, ask if you may check back with him or her in a few months to see if the situation has changed.

It also is possible to get an agent by first getting a job. How? Sometimes independent producers or advertising agencies have their own casting directors and will hire directly, without going through agents. Consult your local phone book or entertainment directory for the listings of independent producers and ad agencies, then call and ask the support staff (not the casting directors, according to the ones we interviewed) for some information.

Find out if and when they hire from the outside. Make sure you ask whether they hire union or nonunion talent. If you are nonunion, for example, and learn that certain people are firm about hiring only union (SAG or AFTRA), don't bother submitting your demo to those people. They will only remember you as someone who wasted their time. If you do get work, you will then have some credits to your name and a track record to point to, which can make agents more inclined to sit up and take notice.

Through online research, you can find Internet sites that, for a nominal fee, allow you to submit an audition and book jobs via the Internet.

DO YOU KNOW PEOPLE WHO ALREADY HAVE AGENTS?

Would they be willing to call their agents and ask them to listen to your demo? If your friends say yes and their agents say yes, that commitment represents one small step for your career and one giant step for mankind.

When you do get an agent, what happens? You will sign a contract. Read and understand every word in that document before you sign it. If you have any questions about anything in the contract, ask them—before you sign it. If the agent cannot explain something to your satisfaction, run it by an attorney—again, before you sign.

The contract should include a "performance clause." Agents generally have ninety days within which they must get you work or the contract can be considered void if you notify the agency and your union(s) in writing.

But considering how busy agents can be, how little time they can devote to any one client, and how many other people are right behind you trying to find an agent, it is in your best interests to get out there and promote yourself.

Once you have a "deal in the making," step back and let your agent do the negotiating. We are not suggesting that you bury your head in the sand and relinquish control of this phase of your career. What we do recommend is that you stay informed but let the agent, who is a professional negotiator, be free to do his or her job—just as you should be free to do yours.

A final word about agents: It may be a lot of fun to jog or play tennis with your agent, but those are pleasant, unexpected, and nonessential extras. The one "must" in any agent/client relationship is trust. You entrust your agent with a significant part of your career; you must be certain he or she will do a good job representing you.

How do you know? Check on the agent's performance. Ask around; find out what other people's agents do for them. But be fair. Remember, you are just one of your agent's many clients, and as such may reasonably expect to have only a small percentage of his or her time. Allowing for that, you can still ask, when your agent does give you your "small percentage," whether it is quality time. Are you being recommended for jobs? Are your demo CDs being sent out? Are you getting any auditions? How are your employment negotiations being handled?

In addition to the overt signs, trust your intuition. If there is any doubt in your mind that your agent does not have your best interests at heart, that doubt will affect your ability to perform. The part of you that is worrying and wondering will not be available to do voice-overs. And if you are operating at less than one-hundred percent, you will deliver less than one-hundred percent—which means you will fall short of your normal high standards of voice-over excellence.

QUESTIONS:

What sort of voices do you like to hear on a demo?

Do what you do best. This is the most important requirement. Do not do something that you do not do brilliantly. Your demo is an opportunity to celebrate you and all that you do well, for commercial demos show your range as it varies with different attitudes for different products with different paces and places that are appropriate. For animation, display your various characters, ages, and their personalities—and don't forget to include a spot that shows your real voice.

Don't put a mom and dad or hero or villain, a little boy or girl, on just because you think you should. If you do not do that character well, then don't do it. As Susan says, "You can make a lot of money being a jack-of-all-trades and just as much being a master of one or two."

I know someone who got an agent without having a demo. Do I really need one to get an agent?

Arlene Thornton answers: "You can get an agent without first having a demo, but this is rare. I like to hear a demo before I decide whether or not to interview the person.

"I did interview and sign someone once who didn't have a demo, but he was referred to me by a client whose opinion I respect. Once the man came in, though, I gave him a very thorough audition to make sure he had professional-level talent.

"Whether or not you have a demo before you get an agent, you definitely will need a demo once you have an agent."

What do agents look for in a voice-over artist?

Rita Vennari, of Sutton, Barth and Vennari, Inc., says, "I look for talent with an instinct to interpret copy creatively and intelligently."

ICM (International Creative Management, Inc.) agent Jeff Danis says, "The world of voice-overs is a complete contradiction, just as is the world of any art. The last thing we need is another announcer, and yet there's always room for another good one. But I mean a real good one.

"It's not enough just to be adequate. You have to be great at what you do to make any type of substantial living. A living that would keep yourself and a top agent interested.

"The ingredients to be 'great,' I feel, are voice quality, reading and interpretation ability of copy, and equally important—a great attitude. For without a great attitude, everything else is worthless."

Arlene Thornton adds, "I like someone who wants to do it right, someone who treats the business professionally. Recently, I heard a young woman's demo. She had very little experience in the business, but I gave her an interview anyway because she filled a gap. I didn't have anyone who sounded like her as a client.

"She came in and was very professional, very motivated. She laid down some copy for me, and I knew she could get work, so I signed her. The very next day she went out and bought a phone answering machine, a beeper, professional labels for her demos, and made herself completely available for auditions. That's what I look for—people who have talent and who treat this business seriously and professionally."

So I can get signed if I don't have a lot of experience. What if I'm nonunion?

Arlene again: "Yes, I'll sign nonunion talent if they're very good. They'll get into a union soon anyway if they're really that good.

"Back to the question of experience for a moment. If you don't have a lot of experience and I give you an interview based on your demo, there are a few things I want to know. Such as, 'Have you taken any voice-over classes or workshops? If so, whose?' 'Have you gotten any work on your own or have you tried to get any?' I want to know if you're motivated. 'Have you been doing legwork on your own? Or have you just been sitting around, waiting to be discovered?' Lazy, I don't need.

"Voice-over is not a part-time job. Sure, you need a survival job to eat and pay the rent until your career really takes off, but make it the kind of job you can leave any time to go on auditions. You must be totally dedicated and available."

I heard agents are inundated with demos. Do they really listen to them?

"I do," says Arlene, "and I keep notes on every demo I listen to. You never know what you'll find.

"When you call for a yes or a no on your demo, ask the agent if he or she can offer you any suggestions for improving your work. You may get some valuable feedback as to what you're doing right and wrong."

Now that I have an agent, how often should I call her?

Arlene answers: "Whenever you have a legitimate question or concern. I don't want my clients agonizing over how quiet it is right now, and 'is it the whole town or is it me?' I do want to hear from my people, but I don't necessarily have the time to call them all. They have to use good judgment and call me when there is a real reason to pick up that phone."

Does an agent mind if I call producers myself?

Arlene doesn't.

"Just don't bug them. You need to have good instincts about this, because nothing will turn off producers or agents faster than someone who won't leave them alone. Even if they like your talent, they'll soon start to dislike you. And they don't hire people they don't like. There are many other nice, talented people out there they can hire."

Another agent says: "I find my relationships with my clients work best when we look at their career as a shared responsibility. I can try to open doors by getting copy into the office and sending them out to auditions, but so much of the legwork depends on how creative they wish to be in selling themselves."

9.

PROMOTING YOURSELF

*H*OW SHOULD YOU PROMOTE yourself?

Any way you can!

In a business that is attracting more and more people, it is becoming increasingly difficult to "get in the door." Your voice-over excellence is certainly the key factor once you do get inside, but getting in—and staying there—can take lots of time and effort on your part.

Having contacts is an important means of promoting yourself. Knowing someone in the business can be most helpful in obtaining information as well as in making other contacts.

If you do know people already in the business, pump them for information. If they have no objections, record your conversations with them. Why? There may be too much information for you to absorb at one time, especially if you are trying to think of other questions you would like to ask. Writing down your questions beforehand helps, but it doesn't allow for the unexpected twists, turns, and tangents in an interview, which can provide a wealth of information you won't want to miss.

Recording a conversation also allows you to hear a professional's words again at a later date. Often, something that you simply glossed over will now JUMP OUT AT YOU. You hear it as if for the first time. And it may well be something you already know, but this time it has particular significance because it solves a problem you are being faced with at this moment.

If your contacts are well-established in the business, ask them if you might accompany them on a job. Not only will you get a feel for a working voice-over environment, but you might also have an opportunity to meet casting directors. Don't impose on your contacts' time or intrude on their working schedules. Just be a sponge and absorb everything you can.

As animation casting and voice director Ginny McSwain says, "The seasoned pros are there for a reason. Experience and success have made them winners. They win parts or spots because they have a unique way of handling audition copy. They have a presence about them—it's evident in their interpretations."

For the beginner, watching professionals work is awesome and inspiring, especially when you understand how complex the whole process is—the process they make look so deceptively simple.

WHAT IF YOU DON'T KNOW ANYONE IN THE BUSINESS? HOW DO YOU MAKE CONTACTS THEN?

Again, any way you can.

Socializing is a good way of promoting yourself and making contacts. In spite of all the work you do alone at home to gain voice-over excellence, the nature of our business is social. But you can't make contacts sitting at home waiting for them to come knocking on your door. Parties and gatherings of all kinds are choice places to meet people in the business. Get yourself invited to as many functions as possible.

Résumés can also be an important promotional tool. We recommend that you keep a professional, up-to-date résumé on hand to submit along with your demo or in place of it. Casting directors are already swamped with demos, and when yours comes in, it may automatically be put on the bottom of the pile. A résumé may attract the attention of someone whose tired ears have "punched out," but whose eyes can still function. Also, from time to time we see ads in the trades (industry trade newspapers or magazines) specifically requesting that voice-over artists submit résumés instead of CDs for a particular job.

A beginner will normally have little, if any, experience to put on a résumé. Do one anyway, and list every related bit of information that might promote you. Make your résumé as distinctive and original as you wish, but keep it simple and easy to read.

Here are two samples. The first is that of an experienced female professional who has an agent. Under "Animation Experience," her cartoon credits are listed. Notice that she includes the names of the studios after the names of the shows.

```
                    T.H.E. PRO
                 CONTACT: A. Gent
             Speak-Easy Voice-Over Agency
               The Agent's Phone Number


                    SAG - AFTRA
```

CURRENT COMMERCIAL AND PROMOTIONAL EXPERIENCE:
This year's credits include:
- Curry's Department Store   (Local Radio)
- Barbara's Chocolate Chip Cookies (National Radio)
- Wagner's Dog Food   (National Radio)
- Blu's Shoe Stores   (National Radio)
- Romano's Pizza   (Network Television)
- Tucker's Long Distance Dialing   (Network Television)
- Numerous Public Service
  Announcements   (National Cable)
- Fall Season Promotional Spots   (Network Television)

Complete list of this year's credits and lists of previous years' credits available upon request.

CURRENT ANIMATION EXPERIENCE:
Current series include:
- *Twitchy Witch; Casey-At-The-Bat* (Boo's Cartoo's)
- *Hummm Dinger; Wing-It*   (The Spelling Bees)
- *Ham Stir; Ms. Mouse The Grouse*   (Rodent Revels)
- *Chick Heard; Dawn Mare O'Dith*   (Animal Olympics)
- *Will O'Tree; Annie Oakley;*
  Sick A'Mour   (Forest Frolicks)

List of past series credits available upon request.

ACCENTS INCLUDE:
- Western American   - British   - French Canadian
- Bronx   - Parisian French - Bavarian
- Brooklyn   - Russian   - Castilian
- Southern American   - Australian   - Chinese

OTHER:
- Extensive A.D.R. experience

The second résumé is for a male beginner who has no representation.

B. GINNER
CONTACT: (Your phone number)

COMMERCIALS:
- Mullin's Small Curd Cottage Cheese   (Cable TV)

OTHER EXPERIENCE:
- Sports Announcer   (Braintrust College Radio Station)
- Public Service   (Braintrust College Radio Station)
  Announcer

TRAINING:
- Susan Blu's Commercial Voice-Over Workshop
- Public Speaking and Debate   (Ona High School)

CHARACTERS:
- Father   - Friendly Next-Door Neighbor
- Child (4-5 years old)   - Not-So-Friendly Policeman
- Child (9-10 years old)   - The Leprechaun
- Shy Teenager   - The Cowboy
- Outgoing "Surfer"   - Refined Southern Gentleman
  Teenager

IMPRESSIONS:
- James Cagney   - The Fonz
- Truman Capote   - Telly Savalas

ACCENTS:
- Bronx   - Cockney

SPECIAL SKILLS:
- Fluent in Spanish

Another way to promote yourself is by using business cards. You can't always carry your demo CD or résumé around with you, nor is it always the right time to present them to a potential contact. Yet you never know when you will meet someone with whom you'd like to leave your name and phone number. Business cards provide a convenient, spontaneous way for the beginner to make a strong, professional impression.

Don't overlook the humble, old-fashioned thank-you note as a way of promoting yourself. Whenever you go on an audition or a job, or whenever a professional does you a favor, write a thank-you note. Not only is this common courtesy, but it also serves to put your name in front of those people one more time. And the more times they see your name, the greater the chances they will think of you when the next suitable job opportunity comes along.

Here are two examples of thank-you notes. The first one is to an agent who listened to your demo and turned you down, but who took the time to give you some constructive criticism.

Dear Mr. Gent,

Thank you for listening to my demo and for taking time out of your busy day to give me some excellent suggestions on how to improve my demo. I welcome and appreciate your input. I do understand that you are not in a position to take on any new clients at this time, but I am holding the good thought that I soon will find an agent as courteous and helpful as you have been.

Sincerely,

In the event you don't find another agent, that letter creates a nice impression, and it leaves the door open a little wider for you to call back and check with Mr. Gent at a later date.

The next note is to a casting director for whom you auditioned.

Dear Mrs. Hornsby,

Just a note to say "thanks" for giving me such a wonderful opportunity to audition yesterday. From the moment I walked in the door, you put me at ease and made the entire experience thoroughly enjoyable.

Thank you for being so considerate.

Sincerely,

Stay informed. Read the trade papers. Split the cost of subscriptions with friends, if necessary, but as a well-informed voice-over artist, you definitely have the edge. You will become conversant with what is going on in the business and will be able to hold your own with anyone. You will also be in a position to seize opportunities as soon as they arise.

Jobs, of course, are often listed in the trades, but don't stop there. Really "get down" and read that paper so you become familiar with names in the business: voice-over artists, casting directors, ad agency executives, etc. Recognizing people's names and being able to comment on their latest accomplishments is an excellent way to please and to be remembered.

Keep up-to-date with movements in the business as well. If you are still looking for an agent or wish to change agents, by reading the trades you can often learn of agencies just starting up or of existing agencies announcing the "grand opening" of a voice-over division. Sometimes the new voice-over division turns out to be one overworked talent agent already on staff who has just been given an additional title. But if the agency has hired or promoted or transferred sufficient staff to really accommodate voice-over artists, this is an excellent time to make contact.

How about a gimmick? Think of something within the boundaries of good taste that will amuse and attract attention. Some people have mailed out calendars with their names on them. Some send out key chains, fly swatters, letter openers, all with their names inscribed. Ideas don't have to be original, either. They can come from anywhere, and you can adapt them to your own needs . . . but remember, talent is the main commodity, so don't spend money on gimmicks if you don't have the funds.

At an early point in Jack Angel's career, he was working at a radio station in the San Francisco area. He wanted to get into voice-over work, and he got an idea for a promotional gimmick from one that had been used by the radio station. He sent out large "Jack Angel Loves You" Valentine posters to a number of advertisers in the area. The posters were beautifully done and carefully mailed in crushproof cylinders.

Jack followed them up a week later with his demo CD. When he went in person from one advertiser's office to the next to introduce himself, he found his face looking back at him from many office walls! He had made quite an impression, a much stronger one than if he had just phoned in to inquire about a job.

Instead of mailing out Christmas cards one year, Susan and her good friend Pat Fraley recorded a delightful Christmas tape that they sent to all their business contacts.

Be creative with your gimmicks. It is the unusual and unique that capture attention, so let your imagination really go wild when you are coming up with ideas for gimmicks. But when it comes time to implement one of your ideas, shift gears and be practical for a moment.

Ask yourself two questions: 1) Can your budget reasonably afford this planned madness? 2) Does your gimmick pass the good-taste test? (This does not mean "Does it taste good?"!) If you get an unqualified yes to both questions, then pull out the stops and go for it!

CD COVERS USED FOR THE ACTORS WONDERFUL DEMOS

10.

THE AUDITION

ONGRATULATIONS! YOU FINALLY HAVE an audition! Acknowledge your success. After all, the fact that you were selected to audition is a success in itself. However, once the euphoria wears off, you may develop a horrendous case of nerves. Logic can tell you that worrying about the audition will not change its outcome and that worry is nothing more than a colossal waste of energy. But try telling that to the family of butterflies that has taken up residence in your stomach. Concentrate. Stay in the process, not in the panic, and approach the audition with professional commitment.

Make a note of the exact time, date, and location of the audition. We suggest you put the information in a small calendar or notebook that you can carry around with you. In that same calendar or notebook, enter your mileage and any expenses incurred in going on the audition. The IRS wants detailed records kept on deductible expenses, and you're much better off logging them in now than scrambling for them in the future.

When you get the call, you will probably be given only a brief description of what the spot will be, such as "a beer commercial." Rarely will you have a chance to look at any copy in advance, so concentrate on preparing yourself mentally and physically for the audition.

At home, run through the Loosening-Up Exercises you learned in Chapter One. As you dress, remember the "noise factor" caused by jewelry, loose change, and certain fabrics. Stay away from perfumes or after-shave lotions. When you get nervous, they can become overpowering for you and for anyone else who has the misfortune of being trapped with you in a small studio.

Don't forget several sharpened pencils for marking the copy, and toss in a few of your business cards as well. Don't give one of your cards to the people who are expecting you; they already know who you are. The cards are for all the "you-never-knows" whom you might run into.

Before you walk out the door, choose something special you will treat yourself to after the audition. It doesn't have to be expensive; it can be as simple as feeding the ducks in the park or buying a Huey Lewis album. What makes it special is that it is a gift from you to you for a job well done.

Think as many positive, happy thoughts as you can to quiet those butterflies. Know that you know what you are doing. Get out of your own way, and let yourself be what you already are: an excellent voice-over artist.

Arriving at an audition at the exact call time is the equivalent of being late. Always leave home in plenty of time to arrive at the audition fifteen to twenty minutes early to prepare. Allow time for traffic and finding a parking place.

On the way over, listen to music that will put you in the best frame of mind. Sing along with it to open yourself up. If you can't hold a tune, sing anyway—loudly. Also on the way over, do some Loosening-Up Exercises again.

When you arrive, remind yourself that you were invited to be there. The people inside truly wish you success; they want you to be the one they are looking for. Sign in and go over the copy using the Basic Process. Mark the copy as needed.

Now is the time to ask the director any questions you might have—such as how to pronounce the name of the product. Don't be unprofessional and take booth time to find out what you should have found out earlier. Casting directors often complain that many people don't seem to care; they just come in, read the copy, mispronounce the product's name, and have no idea what the product does.

A good way to build energy and loosen your mouth is to read the copy once or twice as fast as possible with no inflections whatsoever. Find a quiet, private place to do this and to practice your readings. Duck into the restroom, go out to your car, or just step outside the building for a few minutes, and get comfortable with that copy.

There will probably be an obvious choice and direction regarding the material. Naturally, go with the obvious or with the direction. But also be prepared to do the copy one or two other ways. Remember, don't stop with your decision to read it "softer" or "angrier." Run through the Basic Process and change your answers to one or more of the questions so that your readings will be believably different.

When you are called into the studio, introduce yourself to the casting director (if you haven't already done so), and shake hands. Be spontaneous and sincere in your greeting. Your natural charm and professionalism will win everyone over more quickly than your attempts to be witty and entertaining.

Susan suggests that you "use the moment of introduction to memorize the names and faces of those involved in the casting process.

"I was out one day, and I ran into a very important client. He recognized me right away, but I had no idea who he was. He had to identify himself. It was embarrassing and certainly left a bad impression. From then on, I always made it a point to learn names and faces on all jobs and auditions."

So, that family of butterflies came along with you into the studio, did it? That's perfectly normal. The trick is to use those butterflies and make them work for you by turning "plain old nerves" into "positive energy." You know you're nervous and the casting people know you are, too, so don't waste time trying to conceal or suppress it. Take a deep breath and acknowledge the butterflies, then let them go and retain the energy as you exhale and focus on what you are about to do.

Place your copy on the stand and wait for the engineer to adjust the mic to your height. You will probably then be asked for "a level." Start reading your copy just the way you plan to read it for the real take—same volume, same inflections, etc. This is done so that the engineer can adjust the equipment to best record your voice.

Unless you are recording a double, you will be all alone in the studio, and "they" will be speaking to you over the talk-back from the control room. An interesting phenomenon is that the warm and friendly casting person you just met and shook hands with becomes a terrifying THEY when he/she goes behind the glass of the control room. Keep in mind that it's still the same person.

Okay, but who are all those other people in that booth? There may be more than one casting director, not to mention their assistants, the engineer, and some assorted advertising people such as the copywriter(s), one or two vice-presidents with their assistants, and probably somebody's grandmother. Don't let the number of people in the control room throw off your concentration.

On one audition that included serious subject matter, Molly Ann almost burst out laughing whenever she looked up and saw the staggering number of people crammed into the tiny control room. When one person moved, they all had to move. They looked like a chorus line of sardines. It took every ounce of Molly Ann's concentration not to "lose it."

Why are all those people in there? You can't hear what they are saying, so you figure they're talking about you. That's when you start to wonder if your slip is showing or if your fly is open, and chewing your fingernails up to your armpits seems a comforting thing to do. Well, don't! Knock off those negatives.

Many of those people are there just to observe. Some really have a "say" in the hiring decision. But many others are focusing on the copy—not on you. Consultations go on and on about how to make the copy better. And there's a golden opportunity. If you can deliver a fresh or different reading that will solve their problems, you'll have saved the day and a few people's necks as well. Gratitude, champagne, and jobs will flow your way. When the mic levels have been adjusted, the director or engineer will slate your name. ("This is Susan Blu. Take One.") If you are asked to slate your own name, do so. Then take a brief pause to refocus on your picture of the copy, commit to it, and "let 'er rip!"

On your very first take, as well as on the first takes you do following any changes in choice or direction, go all out with the copy. A director can always bring you back to another level. But if you "start low," you create the impression that this is the best you can do, the most energy and enthusiasm you can possibly generate for the product. No one will ever know how much more you could have done.

Never listen to your own voice, and never let your mind start criticizing your work as you go along. If you stumble over a word, we suggest you stop and start all over again. If you keep going, you might carry the thought of the mistake with you through the rest of the copy and lose your concentration. Worse, you might not get a chance to do another take. So, take a deep and relaxing breath, know you can read that copy perfectly, refocus on your picture, and go for it.

Robert Morse

Once you have done your first take, the director may suggest certain changes in your delivery and ask you to read the copy again. Whether you are given very specific direction or whether all you get is a word, take a moment—and only a moment—to make the adjustment. If you've been practicing the Basic Process, that's all you will need. Which is fortunate: because that's all they will give you. Your time is their money.

Suppose you are given the direction: "Do it again and this time make it sexier." Trying to make your voice sexier is not enough. Don't change the voice—change your attitude and your picture of the copy. Imagine you have just "slipped into something more comfortable" and are about to tell a very special secret to someone you find irresistible. It is late in the evening, and you are totally relaxed and very intimate in front of the fireplace. Commit to that picture, and your reading will melt the mic.

You may get the cryptic direction, "Do it again and give me something else." Here's where one of the alternative choices you made when you first read the copy will come in handy. (If you would like to refresh your memory as to what you did on an earlier take, ask to have that take played back.)

If you receive no direction at all, speak up. Ask if you may do another reading. If they have the time, they will always let you do another take. Often they are grateful that you cared enough about the copy to figure out another way of doing it. Your approach on an additional take may strike them as just the fresh or different one they were hoping for.

BEAU WEAVER WORKS THE MIC.

One mark of a professional is the ability to take direction and work with it. Never, never, never argue with a director about doing the copy his/her particular way. Incorporate the direction into the process. With your mastery of that process, you should be able to deliver believable readings that include any direction.

Sometimes the direction can get a little confusing. On one audition, Molly Ann was asked to "make it lighter, but don't lose the heavy stuff. Punch it, but don't push it. It's a soft-sell, but hit the product name. Warm up the copy, but you don't have to sleep with it. And remember to keep it natural, because this spot is real."

Susan's also heard some good ones: "Let's bring comedy to its knees!" "I don't know what I'm trying to say—act better!" "Somewhere between here and there is the truth." "Act faster!"

Act faster? Go figure.

You can ask for clarification when you are presented with confusing or conflicting instructions. You won't always get it. The best you can do is the best you can do. Never critique your work out loud. That is the director's job. Also, it can destroy the director's confidence in your talent, especially if he or she feels you have done a good reading. If you receive a compliment, say thank you and then— shut up!

Susan didn't always know when to shut up.

"It was early in my career and I was on an audition for a double. We'd done take after take, and finally the director told us: 'That was good. Now, hold a minute.' Well, we held much longer than a minute. After a while I started complaining to my partner, 'We've been here forever! What do they want? I don't think they like me.'

"And a disembodied voice said: 'Yes, we like you. We just need to shorten the commercial a bit.'

"My mic had been on the whole time and I didn't know it! I thought they turned them off when they weren't working with us."

Susan has come up with an effective antidote for the terror of those nail-chewing moments when the people in the control room are talking and shaking their heads—even after the director has told you that the readings were "great."

She used to think, "My readings were really awful. They just didn't have the heart to tell me. And now they can't wait to audition the next person." It finally hit her that, for all she knew, those people were simply talking about the crummy weather or complaining that they hadn't yet received their tax refunds.

From that day on, Susan always "hears their words in my head, and what they're saying is, 'Wow! What a terrific reading that was! I've never heard such a performance! I've never seen such talent!'" These words go beautifully with shaking heads.

Finally it's over. Miraculously, you have lived through it. Thank the people who gave you the audition, and leave on as positive a note as the one you came in on. Don't rush out the door like they're giving away free food down the block. On the other hand, don't linger any longer than politeness and necessity dictate.

Every now and then, as you walk out the door, the thought will hit you: "Now I know how I should have done it!" If you truly feel that this new reading is exactly what they are looking for, walk right back into that studio and politely ask if you might do it for them one more time.

Susan has done this on occasion, saying something like: "I have another approach you might like. Could I do it for you?" The worst they can say is, "No, we don't want to hear it," and you will have lost nothing but a few moments of your time. Just be sure you can trust your feelings. We all get flashes of 20/20 hindsight about "how I could have done it better." Your feelings must be very strong and accurate in order to justify this request for a retake.

Once you make it to your car, climb in, roll up your windows, and yell, scream, shout, laugh, cry. Release all those emotions that have been building up inside you.

You will probably think of at least two hundred better deliveries of your audition on the drive home. That's when the voice-over hangover begins: "They probably

ACTOR SIGNS IN FOR AN AUDITION

didn't like any of my readings. They would've told me if they did. All they said was, 'Thank you. Nice job.' They probably didn't mean that, either!" And it goes on and on and on—if you let it.

Second-guessing is self-defeating. There is no correlation between the praise you receive on an audition and getting the job. Susan swears that whenever she hears compliments—"That was a fabulous reading, just terrific"—she hasn't gotten the job. When all she hears is a lukewarm, barely audible, "Uh, thanks," she gets the job every time.

So when you catch yourself whizzing down a negative mental slalom, put on the brakes and think about something else. Stay positive.

If you get a callback, keep the same professionalism you had before, but don't try to recapture the identical audition. If you focus on the past, you leave no room for the wonderful creative spontaneity that got you the callback in the first place.

QUESTIONS:

I didn't get a callback. What do I do?

Voice actor Jack Angel emphasizes that if you don't get a job from an audition, don't feel that all is lost or that you've lost. Think of it this way: Each job you don't get brings you that much closer to the one you will get. When you do get a job, you're being paid for all those other auditions.

Producer John Westmoreland says: "Casting is not infallible. Take your career seriously, but not the rejections. And don't get discouraged."

Susan says, "One company I'd been the spokes for suddenly decided it was time to do a new campaign with new talent. They put out a call for 'someone who sounds just like Susan Blu,' but they didn't want the *real* Susan Blu. I couldn't understand it; we'd had an excellent relationship over the years, but they just wouldn't see me.

"Finally, the casting director and I cooked up a scheme. I auditioned under another name just to see what would happen. I used the same voice I'd used on all their spots. When they heard that voice, they wanted it—over fifty others. Of course, then we had to tell them the truth.

"They took it well and they hired me. It was risky, though. They could have been angry and never hired me again."

Is there anything "special" I can do to impress casting people?

Ginny McSwain, animation casting and voice director, says, "Talent (especially multiple talents) always impresses me, but personalities and dispositions impress me, too. People who are open-minded enough to take direction, are open to new ideas, and know how to take risks and chances always score points with me. I also like people who are excellent readers and who know how to familiarize themselves instantly with 'cold copy.' What turns me off are people with bad attitudes. It's not hard to hear the 'edge' in a vocal performance when the talent is unfocused or has a bad attitude."

John Westmoreland, producer, told us, "Often it is the cute or unusual line reading that will stand out because no one has heard it before. And it can get you the job."

Susan confirms this with her "delicious" story. "The only line I had for this particular audition was, 'It's delicious!' I read it a few different ways; they thanked me and said goodbye. As I walked out the door, I tossed a very character 'Ooooh, it's delicious' over my shoulder. I was kidding, but the producer yelled: 'Wait a minute! Get back in here and do that again. That's the one we want!'

"Again, on another audition, I was halfway out the door when I called out in a character voice, 'Bye! See you later.' They hired me to do that voice."

Are auditions seasonal?

Commercial auditions often are. In temperate Southern California, there is a flurry of audition activity in late summer and around Christmas time. Why? Advertising executives take refuge out here from the more extreme New York and Chicago weather at those times of the year.

Are auditions (and jobs) regional?

Most voice-over work is done in the "major markets" such as New York, Chicago, and Los Angeles. But don't discount local markets (called "units") for launching your voice-over career. It is often easier to get a few credits by doing some spots for a local radio station. The competition is not as fierce as it is in the major markets, and you may get into a union more quickly this way.

Do I have to belong to a union to get a job?

Not necessarily, and certainly not at the very beginning of your career. Nonunion jobs do exist, but they are generally fewer in number, harder to find, and less lucrative. Many producers have formal agreements with SAG (Screen Actors Guild) and/or AFTRA (American Federation of Television and Radio Artists), the two major unions that represent voice-over artists. As a union signatory, a producer must hire that union's talent.

That's great for voice-over students who are already guild members through other industry activities, but what about the person who belongs to neither union?

At the time of this printing, you can simply walk in off the street, pay an initiation fee, and join AFTRA. SAG will not allow you to do this. You must be hired by a SAG-signatory producer for a union job. A producer can hire outside the union, but the paperwork involved usually discourages this practice. Many voice-over artists who are available for work are already guild members.

If you are hired for a union job, you have thirty days from the date of that first job to do as much union work as you can get, but after that thirty-day period, you must either become a member of SAG or stop accepting union assignments. The union initiation fees (which can be rather steep) and the subsequent dues may seem a financial burden, but the benefits, credibility, and protection a union offers are the best bargains in town.

Our friend and colleague Samantha Paris was able to send one of her talented students, Chuck Kourouklis, of Rancho Mirage, to Los Angeles to audition for three days at the William Morris agency, one of the top voice-over agencies in town. Matt Walter, a William Morris agent, was his booth director for his auditions. Chuck wrote an account of his experiences auditioning for several different products and ad campaigns. Here are excerpts from his journal:

DAY ONE:

I'm in the lobby by 1:30, the appointed time is 2:00, and the lobby is jammed with actors.

Matt brings me the day's copy: an announcer tag, a low-key Californian extolling the virtues of Golden State-grown, a hollering protest leader demanding all the privileges of a Zion's Bank Gold Account, and two computer-game characters for a leading electronics manufacturer.

By the time I'm in the booth, I will have gotten off light with a 100-minute wait—and I would have gladly waited all day. I get in the single's booth, which is about the size of a small closet. There's serious sound-deadening, and the pop screens are compact enough that you have an unobstructed view of the script. And just as I dig in, just like that, the butterflies have all fluttered off.

I lay out my first tries, and after some coaching from Matt, commit a little harder on the second ones. The Zion's Bank protest leader is giving me the hardest time, so I hit that next. I'm broad and big, delivering with the most religious and righteous zeal I can, and—wonder of wonders—Matt coaches me to speed it up.

You gotta understand how big this is for me. It's the truest sign that Voicetrax principles are finally taking root, because the single thing Samantha would tell me most at the beginning was to slow down. So, I do it faster, and Matt saves it. The tag also happens to be for Zion's Bank, so I hit it next in two takes, good to go.

Actually, maybe not the truest sign. Something else important happens. For the first time, ever, I pick up a major clue about the read from the title of the spot. The California-Grown script has the title, "We're Californians. Deal With It." Now what is that if not a pure statement of the writer's intent? After that, there's no question how to hit the line, "We frolic. That's what we do"— your attitude should scream, DEAL WITH IT.

DAY TWO:

It would figure that the one day I'm a touch late should probably have been the day I showed up early. Didn't have any group reads yesterday, but I have 'em today, all right—before I can sit down. Before I even have copy—"Um, Matt, do I get scripts?"

"They're in the booth!"

Absolute zero is defined as -273 degrees centigrade. Yup, about as freezing, moons-of-Pluto-cold as these reads.

On the other hand, we get a rundown, and my part is a cheesy announcer, which I do in my sleep instead of snoring (don't ask). I start off at what I think is a pretty excruciating level of *fromage*, but when we're done with the dry run, Matt actually asks for more. So for the first recorded take, I lay it on thick enough to put Wisconsin out of business, and when the female announcer asks for a restart, Matt tells me to dial it back. Yeah. That's more like it.

Two of those Hormel reads, then Matt asks me to stay for a Shop 'N Save dialogue. I have to shift gears from blaring cable guy to wry understatement, and I do grind 'em a bit; I start out restrained enough, but get a little too big in the middle of the script in the rundown. Matt reminds me that my character is getting interrupted, and I make it more of a point to react this way. I'm a bit rough and need pickups, so I ask for one more go. Cleaner, still not what I wanted, but that's what we had time for.

I'm not over-sure about the TiVo read with the Dr. Phil prototype, so I come on broad; Matt gives me the simple instruction to pull it back and commits the next take. The next deal, a McDonald's read, is supposed to be "young, cool, no deep bass, under 35"—so naturally, I'm like, "Um, dude . . ." But Matt says, "Play it in your upper register and you'll be fine," so I play it in my upper register, and, apparently, I'm fine.

And finally, we hit a Consort Hair Care deal that seems to call for something entirely other than what is being asked for. They actually give four sets of direction on this, none of which seems to hit the mark, but I use one to prepare two reads—neither of which was entirely what Matt thought I should start with, the "very friendly announcer type." I give him the best one of those I could, and then he allows me my option, which is a very dry and droll Joe Friday, Stack-as-Ness interpretation. He's nodding his head on that one.

DAY THREE:

Sure enough, as Sam has admonished and as I knew the instant she said so, I need to bone up on my prototypes; there's this Seinfeld reference for one of my scripts that's completely lost on me. Luckily, some of the actors in the lobby know the prototype and help me out, allowing me to get close enough on my first read that Matt likes the take.

The lobby's thin and time is growing short, so I just start reading through the CBS stuff without any particular regard for who might hear me. By the time I'm done, the fair Kat is staring at me. She says, "You sound fantastic!" And while I'm sure it's more a function of the rumble God gave me than it is of my yet-evolving "madd skillz," I want to propose to her just the same. Just about then, she's whisked away to record her audition. At four P.M. and for the last time on this trip, it's off to the races.

Matt asks right off if I have the Colorado Lottery script. I'm confused at first, but then realize that this was the one with that Seinfeld prototype. So I deliver it in the pedantic tones of a professor lecturing on some terribly important triviality, and as I said earlier, Matt likes the first take.

The Armor All short copy really seems geared for video, and my first read is too understated as a result. Matt coaches a little more energy out of me, and that one's done in the next take.

The Mitsubishi Presidential Pizza script is the second one I've seen that has some key copy hacked off the page, and, unfortunately, for the actual read, I have to abandon the intro I made up about taking a mouthful of your favorite president. The first take is in the general zip code but not quite there; I also check with Matt and find out that they do indeed mean "cooler" instead of "Coolidge" for one particular line, so I give it one more go. I come away with the sense that I might not have played it seriously enough.

Next up is the Uncle Ben's weather report. I'm a veteran meteorologist doing his thing in the studio, and I deliver the lines about eight inches of kabobs and mushroom sauté fronts complete with gestures toward an imaginary green screen and without any irony whatsoever. Matt is moved to observe, "Yep, that's a weather forecast. Good!"

Perhaps my favorite script of the whole bunch, the "Honkey Tonk Haiku," is up next. Don't even know what the product is, but I'm really diggin' the copy. Jack Palance and Rex Allen are the references, but I'm hearing purest Sam Elliott on this one.

Unfortunately, I pay the price for assuming this would be the easiest script. My second take still has a pickup.

And then it's off to Andy's CBS copy. I snap right into the urgency of *The Amazing Race* and the darkness of *CSI*. Too much of that darkness suffuses the Hallmark showcase special, so I lighten it decisively at Matt's cue. After the comedy promos, Matt ventures the opinion that we have a taste of everything in my promo folder.

I have to say, everything goes just exactly as Samantha says it will. The cold reads, the booth direction, the copy typos, the studio logistics—everything, every last detail. A few of my predecessors seemed surprised by the actual confirmation of this. My blasé expectation of it traces back to the one thing beyond a bunch of bad habits that my career has bestowed upon me.

The very first conversation I had with Samantha Paris clued me in that I had encountered someone with an unprecedented level of knowledge in this field. Then the first "Finding Your Voice" seminar propelled me further in three hours than I had managed in the preceding ten years on my own, and each class, each individual instructor, has built further and further on that initial charge.

11

YOUR FIRST JOB

OU'VE BEEN WAITING AND waiting and waiting to hear whether or not you got the job. You don't dare call your agent—again. Just when you think you can stand it no longer, the phone rings and—"Congratulations! You got the job." Make certain you have the correct date, time, and location of the job. Log it in your calendar or notebook.

The Big Day arrives, and there's an International Butterfly Convention taking place in your stomach. What to do? Basically, the same things you did for your audition. Eat something light. Take a relaxing bath or shower. Go through your Loosening-Up Exercises. When you dress, avoid noisemakers, strong perfumes and after-shaves.

If your voice starts to get thick (nerves can produce excess mucus), either suck on a lemon or sip hot tea with lemon in it. If you have a sore throat, a spoonful of honey or hot tea with honey will help. Stay away from dairy products—they induce mucus.

When your mind starts telling you, "You're going to forget everything you ever learned and fall flat on your face," replace that nasty little voice with the thought, "I had what it takes to get this job—I have what it takes to do it."

Leave home in plenty of time to arrive fifteen to twenty minutes early, just as you would for an audition. Make sure the director knows you are there. Get a copy of your script and find a nice, quiet place to go through the Basic Process and prepare for the reading. If you are working with another person, now is the time to introduce yourself and discuss your individual opinions on how the copy should be read.

When you are called in to record, remember to focus your energy on the material, visualize the copy, and commit to your picture of it. You may, although this is rare, have a "buy" on the first take and be told you are free to leave. If so, you will have made a lot of money for a short day's work. But even if your first take turns out to be the buy, the director will usually want a few more done for back-up protection—a variety of takes from which to choose the very best one.

Usually, you will not be kept much longer than an hour for a commercial voice-over. The producers are paying for their time in the studio, and they want to move on to the editing process as quickly as possible.

Occasionally you will have to do take after take after take. Sometimes the ad people are not in agreement. They will often make changes up to and including the last minute. So don't blame yourself for frowns and huddled conversations in the control room.

If it looks like you are going to be in the studio for a long while, conserve your energy; ask for a stool to sit on. Make a quick trip to the restroom. Do a few stretching exercises to restore waning energy. Keep a cup of water handy; you'll need it to keep your mouth from drying up. There will be times when nothing seems to go right. You can't hit on a reading that pleases everybody. Time goes by. Then you give a great reading, but there is a technical foul-up. More time goes by. Then everything is technically perfect, but you flub a line. The ad people start huddling again and shaking their heads.

Just when you feel like you might as well move all your belongings into the studio and notify the post office of your change of address, you will be asked to "do it again—the way you did it the first time."

Don't fall apart! Stay loose, but keep up your terrific concentration. If you can't remember how you did Take One, ask the engineer to play back your first take. Because your readings evoke clear visual images, you will immediately know which picture you used for Take One, and you can easily get back into it. (And it's probably the take they'll buy, too.)

No matter what happens, don't lose your sense of humor. Often you can defuse a tense situation with a humorous word; sometimes all it takes is a smile.

What if you get stuck working with an extremely difficult director? All we can say is that it does happen, but—fortunately—very rarely. When it does, don't let the pressure get to you, and don't lose your professionalism. John Westmoreland worked with a particularly obnoxious director on commercials for a traveling arena show.

"A star had been cast for the production, but the director didn't like her, trust her, or want her in 'his' show. And he certainly didn't want her to do the commercials for it. The director (who was also directing the commercials) brought in his current no-name 'pet' for the TV and radio ads. The director was a very unpleasant, combative man. I spent fifteen minutes in the reception room with him, not knowing who he was. While we waited for the studio to be available, he wouldn't talk to anyone. He wasn't interested in associating with the agency, the star, or the production staff. With just a show of temperament, the star could have easily talked herself out of the whole tour. But she didn't. She had incredible self-discipline and professionalism, and her terrific attitude got her through that difficult time. And, ultimately, it paid off for her."

It's not always the director who tests your mettle. A friend of Susan's did at least fifty takes at one session. Everyone loved his readings except the writer, who kept saying, "It's not right!" after each take. Finally they asked the writer to explain specifically what wasn't right. "It's just not me!" was his complaint.

Your goal is to be remembered as a professional, someone who is pleasant and cooperative to work with.

HOLLY GETS DIRECTED.

John Westmoreland remembers one actor who stayed pleasant and cooperative throughout a nightmare of a session. "He was supposed to be talking excitedly, over lots of traffic noise. We started in the studio and tried to energize him, but he sounded too controlled. He tried and tried, but he just couldn't get it. He was the spokes for the particular product being advertised, so we had to use him. We didn't really want to call in someone else because he'd always performed well before, but this time he was having difficulty with the copy.

"We wanted that slightly hysterical edge that comes from having taxis narrowly miss you. So we ended up putting him on a traffic island between two very busy streets. We ran the cable through the crosswalk and gaffed it to the street. I was standing on the sidewalk, four car-widths away, giving him hand signals. We got hysteria.

"We also got spots that could not be cut, because the sound effects were too heavy to match. So, not only did he have to give us excitement, he also had to be letter-perfect from beginning to end, and his timing had to be exact. He was a good actor and he did his best. All day. No complaints, no temper. His attitude made all the difference."

On your way out, remember to again thank the people you worked with. When you get home, write the producers a thank-you note. This thoughtful gesture serves to put your name in front of the "powers that be" one more time. Also, you may ask to have a copy of your spot mailed to your agent for inclusion on your demo.

QUESTIONS:

When do I get paid for doing a job?

If you do a nonunion job, you often will be paid immediately after the recording session.

If you are union, the producers are required to send out your check within twelve working days of your employment. However, by the time your agent takes out his or her ten percent and sends you a check for the balance, the entire process can take anywhere from three to five weeks. If an ad agency cancels a session, for whatever reason, the talent still must be paid.

There is always the "other form of payment," which money can't buy: the thrill of hearing your spot on the radio or watching it on television. There's no way to put a dollar value on this one—it is such an incredible high!

What are "buyouts"?

Arlene Thornton fielded this one:

"Complete buyouts (a flat, one-time fee paid for voice-over services) don't exist in union situations. Except for industrial narrations. Those are buyouts. Often, so is nonunion work. But where the talent is union and identifiable (as opposed to hand models, for example), payments and residuals go in thirteen-week cycles."

Are jobs seasonal?

John Westmoreland answers: "They can be. But it's not really fair to expect the production company to produce a spot in the season for which it is intended. We need a reasonable amount of lead time to prepare for the session. On the other hand, if you record far in advance of the target season, you aren't being fair to talent either, because you must put a hold on them. They are paid not to record copy for a competing product until their spots are run. But then you're paying actors not to do what they really want to do—act."

12.

A FEW FINAL THOUGHTS

OR "OUT OF THE BLU" & "MULLIN' IT OVER"

*V*OICE-OVER SUCCESS IS ATTAINABLE; voice-over techniques can be learned and success can be achieved. Animation casting and voice director Ginny McSwain tells us that "voice-over is an art form unto itself. It is a craft that can and must be learned, just as on-camera techniques must be acquired. To succeed, professional actors must train to do voice-overs, just as fresh or 'green' talent must also train. Training, plus desire and commitment, will result in success."

Realistically, there will be times when you won't get the job. There may even be long stretches of time when you won't get any jobs. Voice-over artist Paul Kirby holds onto one thought after each turn-down: "It's all just a matter of selection, not rejection."

That thought helps ease the pain during those long dry spells. The one job you do get is the payoff for all the preparations you have done and all the auditions you have gone on.

As writer/producer Larry Belling says: "An attribute required by successful voice talents is a very thick skin. We know several pretty good voices who have auditioned over a thousand times and not landed one job. The competition is fierce!"

Don't let the frustrations end the game for you. As casting and voice director Andrea Romano states, "You must have the stamina to keep knocking on those doors!"

Be positive. Doubts have a sneaky way of creeping up on you at the worst possible times. These times correspond to your weakest and, therefore, most vulnerable moments.

One technique we use to stay positive is visualization. If you have mastered this technique for doing voice-overs, you will have a head start in using it this particular way. When you get a call for an audition, picture yourself actually going on the audition. See yourself getting ready for it and going through all the preparations we discussed. See yourself driving to the audition, arriving, signing in, and going over your copy. Imagine yourself doing an excellent reading of the copy and getting the job. If you can see something happening, you accept the possibility that it could happen.

Director Gordon Hunt discusses fear in his book *How to Audition* (HarperCollins). Although he only briefly touches on voice-over auditions, Gordon's extensive treatment of audition fears is well worth reading.

Don't downplay the importance of learning acting techniques regarding voice-overs.

Voice director Ginny McSwain's opinion: "Acting comes first, the voice comes second, and then the acquired technique for voice-over ties the two elements together. People who merely mimic, do impressions, or make funny sounds must be able to sustain one or more characters throughout an entire script.

MOLLY AND THE VERY TALENTED
ED ASNER.

Stand-up comics who are not actors have a great deal of trouble staying in character for any length of time; they are more used to a spontaneous, rapid-fire delivery for a limited period of time."

"Acting is very important," says producer John Westmoreland, "and in slice-of-life spots that require you to sound natural, you must lose the 'polish' that often comes with certain kinds of stage or on-camera training. A good acting class will give you the proper techniques without the artificial polish."

Always give credit where credit is due. Acknowledge those who have helped you, but don't forget to congratulate yourself on each step you take up the ladder. Recognition may come from others, but it means so much more if it comes to you from you. Only you know all the hours of work and sacrifices you made to become an excellent artist. It was your discipline, your efforts, and your talent that made it happen. Respect yourself and your talent.

John Westmoreland has a healthy respect for voice-over actors because, "I did a free political spot once, and it really struck me what talent is paid for—their professional training. My nerves made my throat constrict, and my voice kept getting higher. You get what you pay for."

As you move up in the ever-widening circle of voice-over professionals, you will have the pleasure of meeting some of the most generous and giving people in the whole world. We have quoted a number of them in this book; others may be heard on the *Word of Mouth* CD. They are the first to celebrate your successes, and will gladly share their experience and tips with you. Secure in the knowledge of their own excellence, they have no need to distance themselves from "the competition," whom they regard as friends and colleagues in the business.

WHAT MAKES A "WINNING" VOICE-OVER ARTIST?

We asked several prominent voice-over artists for their insights, which they kindly shared with us.

B. J. Ward: "I try to do everything I can to test my limits. Seasons of summer stock—doing a show each night, rehearsing another play during the day, with children's theater on the weekend. Improvisational training and theater. Letting myself go on stage with no planned script and playing the improv games. Trusting myself and my fellow actors.

"Singing lessons. Learning my vocal range and strengths, how dependable an instrument I had, or have. (It's an ongoing process.)

"Voice-over workshops. Learning to work with my voice, reading lots of copy, getting the words up off the paper, making them mine, and making my choices quickly.

"I learned a tremendous amount teaching voice-overs. Doing stand-up and my own nightclub act. It all helps define who you are and what it is YOU have to offer. It helps to have a little talent and some good fortune. And while you're waiting . . . be happy. Appreciate what you have at any given moment. BE FUN TO BE AROUND."

Jennifer Darling: "The 'voice' is the major part of the whole mechanism that enables the actor to express herself. So I figured I'd better deal with it—'the voice'—and once I did, I realized what a gift my voice was. I started dancing at the age of three, acting lessons at ten, and singing—imitating singers and doing dialects—at eight. At fourteen I had a problematic appendectomy and had to stop dancing for a bit. I got very involved with singing, then went to New York to cut a record, appeared on *Ted Mack's Amateur Hour* and won. From then on, my voice became the center of my attention—I knew it was unique and would always help me to 'win.' At Carnegie Mellon University, I majored in Drama and also studied every aspect of the voice from dialects to Shakespeare. I toured the country doing repertory and found myself in New York, where I appeared 'on' and 'off' Broadway for seven years, doing Shakespeare for Joseph Papp, appearing in television for the *David Frost Revue*, and also doing a soap opera; always working, studying, watching, listening and hopefully learning. When I came to California, I got involved with 'nighttime' television. This was a new challenge for me and of course 'the voice'—a medium that deals with confinement and economy.

"TV and radio voice-overs were always fascinating, but then came animation. I could dig down deep and find all the characters that were lurking about. I could try them, stretch myself in another new way, and get back to the beginnings of the theater and then some . . . and not be carried away for it. Here was another medium; all those artists sitting behind microphones doing a play; an outrageous play. I found yet another home, a new home in which to create. The world of animation—the voice knows no limits there. Trust yourself, study, follow your instincts, and know that you are unique—listen to your inner voice so that you can win with your outer voice."

Dick Gautier: "I'm fortunate in that I divide my time between TV, movies, stage, and the field of voice-overs and animation. When I was in my early twenties, before going 'legitimate,' I was a standup comedian whose stock and trade was weird sounds, offbeat impressions, and various dialects. These strange talents lay dormant while I pursued film and TV roles, but when the world of animation and voice-overs beckoned, I quickly resuscitated the voices and dialects, and now I'm having a terrific time doing voices for heavies, heroes, and a host of bizarre creatures."

Linda Gary: "I have been an actress since I was a child, but I have only concentrated on voice-overs (commercial, theatrical, and cartoon) for the past twelve years. My achievement has mainly been due to my determination to 'be better,' to work hard, and enjoy that work. If I had to list my beliefs in what helped me attain whatever success I have achieved, I would have to say: pay attention to the business acumen of being an actor, acknowledge those who help you along the way, maintain a professional attitude, be courteous to your fellow actors, listen to the director, and be able to change instantly when the direction changes. Don't rest on your past characters—create new ones (the car is a great place to create), don't whine, don't nag, and have fun!"

If the Basic Process and other techniques you learned in this book work for you, then don't abandon them when the going gets easy. They worked for you in the past, and they will continue to work for you in the future.

Never lose sight of the fact that voice-over is, as Brian Cummings says, the process of "becoming." Every piece of copy offers you the opportunity to use your creative energy to become a unique and different speaker for a particular product.

Voice-over is also "the process of becoming" in the sense that you must keep nurturing your talent if you wish to continue to improve and grow. If, at some point, you feel you have learned or have done it all, your talent will begin to stagnate.

Ginny McSwain feels that ongoing, constructive workshops are an excellent place to nurture your talent. "Workshops provide a vocal workout, using a variety of exercises. You don't just learn 'Voice-Over 101' and then 'have it.' The best workshops and classes push the artist to grow and to learn how to compete and how to win jobs. Workshops with guest speakers who are established in some area of the voice-over field allow you to get a feel for 'what's out there,' plus learn invaluable information from the speakers' own experiences."

So, continue to study and to practice, be persistent, and—above all—be positive!

After some additional words from our generous contributors, it will be time for you to put this book down and concentrate on internalizing the entire voice-over process, so that all the techniques we discussed become second nature to you. With enough practice and repetition, voice-over excellence will become yours—instinctively and naturally.

Remember: The only limits you'll experience are the ones you place on yourself. And you have our sincerest and best wishes for unlimited success!

KNOW WHAT
THE PROS KNOW

N THIS NEW EDITION of *Word Of Mouth* we wanted to again ask the very top professionals in different facets of the industry their answers to two important questions.

First: "What advice would you give a voice actor getting into the business?"

Second: "What are the ingredients that make up a great voice actor?"

Deborah Forte, the president of Scholastic Media, who has been instrumental in creating brilliant entertainment for children all around the world, had this to say:

> Voice acting is like compressing all five senses into one. Through sound we need to be able to imagine a complete person. Those who do it well can convey everything through their voice performance—attitude, age, gender, personality, etc.

Kelly Garner, the owner of Pop Art Management, helped create the voice-over department at Abrams Artists Agency in Los Angeles, and has been influential in establishing the careers of many voice-over artists. Here are his thoughts:

When I got into the industry, everyone said an interesting voice is the place to start. So I loaded up on actors with deep voices, quirky voices, raspy voices, nasal voices, and so on. But, what I found was that an actor with an interesting voice could sometimes gain employment . . . but an actor with an opinion on life and how it was to be lived made the most money.

Some actors just come in to the voice-over world with a personality that is "bookable." When they read the copy and the voice directions, they know how they feel about it, and can convey the message at its simplest level. We are compelled to hear what these actors have to say because they have a particular attitude and opinion. This is not to say that there is not a great deal of training or practice behind the voice-over art, but if you've got a point of view in life, this is the time to use it.

When I meet actors in my office, I can immediately tell if they would need a lot of training to find their opinion, or if it just comes with their personality. I had one actress come into my office and tell me her agency would not take a chance on her trying to cross over in to the voice-over industry. This particular talent had been doing films, television, and on-camera commercials since she was seventeen (and she was now in her thirties). But that's not what interested me. She was interesting because she was earthy. She viewed life from a very specific and grounded place. She saw things as simple and enjoyable. There was a bonus, too: Her voice was also earthy. She started auditioning for me, and the next thing you knew, she was the voice of a national car spot, then radio spots came, then campaigns for banks, dot-coms, underwear—you name it, she got it.

We've all got a "take" on life. Some people see this world as a real pain (that person is great for the funny partner reads where you need sarcasm), and some people are so happy to be alive you think they float when they walk (that person is wonderful for the overly perky office worker who irritates our sarcastic character). Some people are just cool sounding and others are just geeky . . . and all those qualities are bookable. If you can harness your view on this world and vocalize it, you are taking the first step in the right direction.

Here's Kelly's advice to new people getting into the business:

DO NOT listen to any agent, casting director, producer, or so-called figures of authority who tells you to give up on your dream if they haven't heard you read, listened to your demo, or simply have not taken the time to find out who you are as an actor. People like to go for the negative a little too fast in this town. It is common to hear them say "no" before they actually judge a new voice-over artist on their real merit. This attitude has nothing to do with you. The voice-over business is fast and people have a lot on their plate, but I promise, if you've got the voice someone is looking for, they will stop what they're doing and pay attention.

DO listen to these same people if they are giving you advice and have studied your performance or voice-over demo. If you were lucky enough to have them audition you, teach you, or produce your demo, then they will have valid points. Sometimes this business can really be the wrong business for you. Actors can sink a lot of money into trying to start a voice-over career, but if your resounding feedback is negative, don't ignore it. These professionals (most of the time) know what they are talking about. This should be your cue to go pursue the things you are better at. And, if the feedback is positive, go for it. Persistency is everything.

Audu Paden has been turning big pencils into little ones profession-ally for more than twenty years. Currently directing the animated *Stuart Little 3* feature, he has produced and directed more than 150 hours of television programming. Just some of his producing and directing credits include *Spider-Man, Animaniacs, Tiny Toon Adventures, Rugrats,* and *The Simpsons.* He has received the Peabody award and two Daytime Emmys.

Audu's advice about entering the business of animation:

From a practical point of view, I need to keep expenses low. Since I am permitted to have one actor play two roles without additional cost, I will often cast single-line parts or secondary roles from the primary cast. (If you are asked to do a third voice, you should receive a ten percent increase.)

Thus, when casting, I often look for actors who can perform multiple voices that sound sufficiently different, so that the audience should not recognize it as the same actor.

Typically I will cast a second or third voice at the recording, by asking the most likely actors in the existing cast to try out a line or two. If this happens to you, feel free to offer two or three different voices. One of them might be what the director likes. If you can generate a reputation for having of spectrum of voices and accents, I promise that you will be cast more.

Audu continues:

Most of the work I do requires realistic voices in dramatic situations. As an actor, don't go outside the comfortable range of your natural voice. If it sounds put-on and phony to you, it will to the audience as well. Look at the script, understand the meaning, then try to "lift the words off the page." This means getting away from the rhythms of reading; put yourself in the moment that your character is living. Don't rush. Think about the punctuation—typically these are the moments when your character is thinking of what to say next. Remember, your characters always take themselves seriously.

It is also important to remember that the visual performance is created after the vocal performance. Animators will listen to a recording of your acting again and again to get information about a character's acting beats, gestures, and mood. Since none of the subtle clues of acting that are communicated by the face and body is present, sometimes you need to exaggerate the dynamics of your voice to help the process. Your director should let you know how far to push this for each project. Stylistically, this can mean looking for contrasts within a phrase and emphasizing them. For example, you may contrast the first half of a phrase to the second by adjusting volume, pace, or pitch at the transition point of the phrase. If I do not hear enough range in a delivery of a line, I sometimes ask an actor to deliver a line twice, in different ways. I will then edit between the two later at the studio to artificially sculpt the dynamics of the delivery.

Finally, do not be afraid to pause and gather your thoughts before delivering your next line—I can always trim the gap out. I want you to sound good.

Ellen Cockrill is a studio executive who has worked in creating such projects as *Woody Woodpecker*, *The Mummy* (television series), *Curious George* (television series), and various pilots, including *Johnny Bravo*, *The Cowardly Dog*, and *Cow and Chicken*. Her advice is stellar.

> First and foremost, people who want to do voice-over acting need to develop their acting craft. Great voice-over acting requires great acting. Second, they need to learn the specific craft of voice-over acting—of how to put a whole performance into their voice. And third, they need to meet the people who cast the roles. What I recommend to actors who tell me they're interested in voice-over work is to take a voice-over acting class from a professional in the business—preferably someone who casts shows.
>
> A great V.O. performer is a great actor first and foremost, and can put a whole performance into their voice. They also take direction well. Sometimes a director has a specific thing they're going after, and the best actors easily make little adjustments. A great V.O. performer also is versatile, a quick study, and easy to work with. When we're in a recording session there's usually a lot to do in a little time. The great actors nail the performance quickly. Also, often when we're recording new characters, we need to find the voice in the session. The best actors can do a few different versions of a character.

Jamie Simone, dialogue director and casting director, has directed hundreds of episodes of animation as well as many animated films, including: *Spider-Man*, *Totally Spies*, *Casper*, *The Incredible Hulk*, *Bratz*, and *Iron Man*. Jamie offers the following:

> Having a great natural voice or the ability to create voices isn't enough. Acting is the key. Immerse yourself in what you want to do. Study your craft. Make sure you are prepared for your auditions. Learn good mic technique. It may take some time to get where you need to be, but if you are good, someone will take notice and you will find work.
>
> Great animation actors are fearless. They are not afraid to think out of the box while still staying on line with the animation director's vision of the character. They have the ability to make large or small adjustments in both performance and voice.

Jeff Danis, Senior Vice President of ICM, shared great words of wisdom with us in the first edition of this book. When writing the present edition, we again posed our questions to him, and he added the following insights.

> My advice to new people getting into the business is to listen to TV and radio commercials. REALLY LISTEN . . . and if you think you are as good as they are, then take a class. When you are ready, make a professional demo to send into agents. But, please only make the demo when you are ready. DON'T RUSH THE PROCESS.
>
> The great ingredient is, first and most important, acting ability. Without that, no great voice alone will really make the difference. Oh, sure, with a great voice you might get some work, but it will not give you a career. Only good acting will. And, after that, patience. This is a long-term commitment and, like any career, it doesn't always happen because you think you're ready. You are in it for the long haul, so be patient.

Grace Benn, Vice President of Development of Sony Pictures Television, had this to say:

> Most of the actors we hire are found through the voice directors we hire. So perhaps the best advice I can give is to get to know voice directors. Take classes taught by working voice directors. Work on your craft and have a number of voices and dialects that you can call upon in an audition. Come to auditions prepared with a couple voices based on what you think fits the character breakdown. Never be afraid to ask to try something again. Be fearless. Have fun. And probably most important, be nice. Be someone that everyone wants to work with again. It's a profession where nice guys (who are talented and work hard) can finish first.

What ingredients make up a great animation actor in your opinion?

> Great acting ability; the ability to convey the emotion of a scene with only the use of the voice. In animation, the voice record is done prior to the animation, and it is the recording that helps

guide the storyboard artists as to the emotion of the characters in each scene. If the acting is flat, then the designs will be too. Versatile voice; the ability to create and consistently repeat numerous characters who sound vastly different in tone, pitch, cadence, and/or dialects. Great animation actors can convincingly portray several characters in the same episode and never have the audience realize it's only one actor. Responsible. Fun. Great personality. Fearless. Did I mention strong acting skills and a versatile voice? Ability to take direction. Willingness to take direction. Intelligence. Professional.

Marsha Griffin is an Emmy-nominated writer and story editor who has been working in television animation since 1997. Her credits include the animated television series *Godzilla*, *Men in Black*, *Starship Troopers*, MTV's *Spider-Man*, *Jackie Chan Adventures*, and *The Life and Times of Juniper Lee*. Marsha told us:

> Bottom line: If you want to work in television, you need to *watch* television. All kinds of television—animated and live-action. That may sound like a given, but you'd be surprised how many writers, actors, and executives will tell you they don't bother tuning in to anything, even their own shows, as if it's a badge of honor rather than a tacit admission that they haven't prepared for their jobs. You need to watch the shows, see and hear the performances of other actors, and listen to the words of other writers to appreciate the business as a whole. Ultimately, if you think you're too good to waste your time watching television, then you'll never be good enough to work in it.

> From my perspective as an animation writer/story editor, there is one ingredient to great animation acting that many people forget: You're only as good as your material. The relationship between the actor and the writer should not be underestimated. That's because writing is almost always a solitary experience, with long periods of time devoted to creating characters, who speak only in our minds. But when an actor finally says those words, embodying them in the flesh for the first time—trust me, it's a huge thrill. Unfortunately, some actors tend to forget that there's a person behind those words—somebody who created them so your character could exist.

So do yourself a favor and follow a few simple tips. First, when you get a script, read the whole thing—NOT just your own lines. We put a lot of time into making the script work as a whole, and you should have the same vested interest. Second, try to refrain from telling the writer that "my character would never say that." Your character CAN and DOES say that—we know because we wrote it. And finally, never complain to the writer about how many lines you have in the script, because at next week's record session, your character will suddenly become mute.

Suzie Peterson, Executive Vice President, Production, Universal Home Entertainment Productions, is very clear on what she looks for:

As a studio executive, I'm always juggling a lot of projects at once, so I don't have time to screen voice-over candidates, or even listen to individual voice reels. No matter how clever or appealing the presentation, it's wasted on me. I rely completely on casting and voice directors to put together auditions. So, take classes and get your demo to agents and voice casting directors. Be willing to audition for everything, and be a good sport. I've always felt as if the voice-over business, especially in animation, runs on high spirits. Everyone is just sitting there, but the atmosphere has to stay energized. If you bring a lot of positive energy into the sessions, along with your great talent, of course, you'll always be welcomed back.

The greatest performers for me are either incredibly versatile or specialized in a way that's unforgettable. Undoubtedly there's more work for the versatile. I think it's very hard work to communicate everything with your voice, without benefit of body language. You can't rely on your good looks or physical methods at all, so it's an art of intense focus that requires ability and skill more like an athlete's than a screen or stage actors. You really have to have the goods—no sliding by on your looks. There are lots of movie and TV "stars" who are flat, uninteresting, and even unrecognizable when they do voicework—they're hired for their marketing appeal, and it usually hurts the project. Every bit of nuance matters, and it all has to come through that voice. The great ones are wonderful actors, mimics, comedians, singers, charismatic personalities, and they just have that energy that feels bottomless.

GLOSSARY

"accent it" — Add stress or emphasis to your reading of a syllable, word, or phrase.

active commercial — Calls for an aggressive delivery. It's also known as a "hard-sell."

"add life to it" — Your reading is dead. Give it CPR (Concentration, Positive energy, and Revive it!).

announce booth — See "studio."

A.D.R. — Stands for "Automated Dialogue Replacement" in a film. (We've also heard it called "Automatic Dialogue Replacement.") It's a more modern technology than looping. All the sound readers and the projector are kept in absolute synch as you project forward or back up. Instead of having to do anything in one continuous take or having to cut the picture into loops, you can actually take the film as it's edited to be seen, back it up on the projector, and start replacing lines section by section. You can literally punch in any time you want to. It's a magnetic recording, and it's capable of doing a very silent job of punching in without any clicks or pops.

attitude — How your character feels about a particular product. Also, how you feel about a particular situation, be it an interview, an audition or a job. A good attitude can get you remembered kindly all over town.

background noise — The sounds of those activities that are going on simultaneously with the spoken words of the commercial. They are either recorded live along with the copy or are mixed in later in post.

Basic Process — Our sure-fire three-step method for delivering the most exciting, believable readings: Focus your energy on doing the voice-over, visualize the copy, and commit to that picture of it.

"be real" — Keep your delivery as true-to-life as possible. Add a genuine or sincere quality to your character.

"billboard it" — Highlight or emphasize your reading.

break character — Inadvertently becoming another character or losing the one you were. Happens to the best of us when our concentration's thrown off.

"bring it up/down" — Increase/decrease the intensity of your reading. May also refer to raising or lowering your volume.

bumper — Extra recording or post time in a studio.

buy — As in, "That's a buy." That take is the one they want.

buy-out — A one-time fee paid for your voice-over services. Typically seen in nonunion situations and industrials.

cadence — Having to do with how the words are strung together in phrasing; how breaks are placed in between words.

callback — A request for you to go back for another audition. (Okay, so maybe you can't open the bottle of champagne just yet, but you can start chilling it.)

"cans" — A nickname for headphones.

CD — Compact disc, which is currently the favored format for submitting voice-over demos.

character — That person you've chosen to be in a commercial. Even as an announcer, you must choose to be a Particular Announcer to do the best possible readings.

"color it" — Find the magic in the copy; give it shades of meaning.

"cones" — Another nickname for headphones.

conflict — You would be "in conflict" if you did two commercials for the same type of product. A big no-no in the industry. A conflict can also mean that you sound like someone else. Agents may turn you down because they already have a client who has your sound, and signing you would represent a conflict.

copy — The text in commercials or animation. Also called a "script."

control room — Where the engineer, producer, client, etc., are located during a session. Also called the "booth."

cuts through — When your voice nicely overrides the music and sound effects. It cuts through, but doesn't demolish the other effects.

dead air — What happens when a voice-over pause is too long.

demo — A demonstration of your talent. It consists of various spots, usually one to two minutes in length, that showcase a voice-over artist's range and skills. Demo categories are commercial, animation, promo, and narration. A sales tool, it serves as your remote audition for agents and casting people.

dialogue — The text in the script.

double — A commercial calling for two voice actors. Also called a "two-person spot."

donut — Copy at the beginning and/or the end of a spot. It "wraps around" the body of the commercial, which changes from spot to spot while the donut is always the same. Example: "And now at Donna's Discount Delight . . . (body of the commercial) . . . New for you from Donna's."

drop — Lowering the volume or intensity of the reading.

dry mouth — What you get when you've been at the mic too long, or because your nerves are acting up.

dubbing — Dubbing really has nothing to do with replacing dialogue tracks. It is actually the process of mixing down the picture or the spot, and it's something the engineers do once the voice-over talent has gone home. Over the years, however, dubbing has become synonymous with looping. Some people also refer to the dialogue replacement in a foreign film as dubbing.

edge — The quality your voice takes on when you intensify your attitude.

"endow the copy" — Using our Basic Process to give the copy a special something that will make it your very own.

energy age — The age you "think" so that your character, regardless of his or her chronological age, can always give a fresh reading.

equalizer — A machine with treble and bass controls. Engineers use it to thin out or give bottom end to your voice, which can make your character seem, for example, more important or sexier.

fade-in/fade-out — What happens to the sound of your voice when you turn your head away from the mic and back again while you are speaking.

"Father Clarity" — (This is not someone who is called in to administer the last rites to dead air.) Often directors ask talent to watch their diction. Out of numerous requests to "read the copy with more clarity" has come the short-hand expression "Father Clarity."

"fix it in the mix" — When mistakes are not handled or caught while the talent is still in the studio, the engineers must correct them in post.

fluctuation — How often your voice goes up and down. If you have no fluctuation in your voice, you are speaking in a monotone.

Foley stage — A special soundstage used for source sound effects. Boards on a Foley stage floor may be raised to provide access to areas filled with different substances, such as loose gravel, sand, or pavement. Various props may also be found on a Foley stage. The process itself involves watching on-screen characters and matching appropriate noises to their actions. Footsteps, glass breaking, doors and windows opening and closing are all examples of noises that can be produced on a Foley stage. (Susan once saw someone working on a Foley stage, and as he walked across it, he had his hand cupped to his ear like Gary Owens!)

gate — Another name for dialect.

"give me a level" — Start reading your copy exactly the way you plan to read it for an actual take. This is done so the engineer can adjust the equipment to best record your voice.

go up for — To audition or be considered for a job. "I went up for a Curry's Department Store" means that you auditioned for that spot. "I'm up for a Wagner's Dog Food" means you already auditioned and they are now considering you for that spot.

group reads — Commercials calling for more than two voice actors.

hard-sell — See "active commercial."

high point — The last beat or resolution to the mini-play that is in a piece of copy.

hold — You are "on hold" when you are being paid not to do certain types of spots because the spot you recorded has yet to run and would be in conflict with the others.

house minute — An agency's demo. It includes condensed versions of the clients' demos, usually separated into male and female sections.

inflection — The raising or lowering of the pitch of your voice. Generally used for longer phrases, rather than a one- or two-word ad.

intensity — A focusing of your energy that is reflected in your character's attitude.

"keep it fresh" — When you're reading the copy for the twenty-fifth time, give it the energy of your very first take.

laundry list — When there are lots of adjectives in a piece of copy.

lay it down — Record a piece of copy.

"less sell" — Make it a softer spot.

live mic — The mic is on. And can pick up anything you say. And will deliver it straight to the ears of the producer, the engineer, the clients, and anyone else who is crammed into the control room. (And it may come back to haunt you, as it did Susan. She used to spit out some interesting four-letter words when she flubbed a line. When she went to an important client's Christmas party, they played a tape of her "outtakes." "I almost died of embarrassment," she says. "Now I watch my mouth.")

live tag — One- or two-line copy delivered live by a DJ at the end of a prerecorded spot.

looping — The older technology of dialogue replacement in a film. A scene is cut into pieces, each piece being the length of a particular line. The pieces are joined into loops and mounted on a projector so you, as the looping talent, can see them over and over. You look at the screen and it's black. Then a white line runs across it from screen left to screen right. When it hits the right edge of the screen, the scene will come up. You'll hear and see how the original line was spoken. At the end of that line, you'll go back to black and the white line will again make its way across the screen. This enables you to establish a matching rhythm to what you are looping.

major markets — Cities such as Los Angeles, Chicago, and New York, where the majority of voice-over work takes place.

"make it flow" — Make your delivery smooth. Avoid choppy, staccato readings.

"make it intimate" — Do you really need us to tell you what this means?

"make it yours" — Personalize the copy. Endow it.

mix — The result of a mix-down.

mix-down — Combining the various voice, sound effects, and music tracks into one.

"more energy" — Punch it up—you're dragging your vocal tush.

"more sell" — Billboard the copy.

multiple — A commercial calling for more than two voice actors.

nerves — As in "I've got a bad case of . . . ." They usually start doing their thing before an interview, an audition or a job. They are something to leave outside the door when you go in for the interview, audition, or job. Your best bet is to turn them into positive energy and let them work for you.

one-on-one — See "intimate."

overlapping — In a double (or multiple), starting your line a fraction of a second before your partner finishes his or hers.

pace — The speed with which you read the copy.

paper noise — This is the sound of paper being fluttered and/or otherwise moved about in front of a mic. When recording, do not move your script pages—put them on a script stand!

passive commercial — A soft-sell. It calls for a more laid-back approach.

pause — A break in between syllables, words, or phrases. Remember to make it a short break or you'll have dead air.

phase interference — What happens when sound reflects off your script and into the mic.

phonemes — Very small units of the sounds we use to make up words. Example: the "r" of the word "rat."

"pick up your cue" — Come in faster on a particular line.

pick-up session — An additional recording session to record individual lines out of context either for backup protection or because they weren't right the first time—for whatever reason. Sometimes an entire script may have to be redone.

pitch — The ups and downs we hear in normal conversation. The musical level at which you speak.

placement — Where the voice is coming from, i.e., the nose, the chest, the stomach, etc.

plosive — A small burst of wind into the mic. Plosives are usually caused by voicing hard consonants.

pop filter — A screen, usually circular in design, that is positioned in front of a mic to eliminate pops.

pops — Noises resulting from hard consonants spoken directly into the mic. They sound like short, sharp bursts from an air gun.

post — The post-production session that starts once the voice-over talent has completed the recording session.

pre-life — What was going on with your character just before the actual copy starts.

promo — A promotional spot. It promotes a product or, more often, a service.

"punch it" — Give the copy more energy.

"push/don't push" — Give the copy more/less energy.

read against the text — Reading a line with an emotion other than the one it would ordinarily call for.

residuals — Continuing payments you receive each time your spot is run. Usually divided into thirteen-week cycles.

rhythm — The cadence of the speaking voice.

"romance the 'phone" — Make friends with that mic. It is your only link to that particular person you're speaking to.

run-through — Rehearsal of the copy before an actual take is done.

scale — The established union wage rate for a recording session.

"sell it" — Billboard or punch it.

session — A recording session. The period of time in a studio during which the voice-over talent lays down the copy.

SFX — Stands for "sound effects."

"shave it by . . ." — Cut a certain amount of time off your delivery.

signature — Your vocal signature are those qualities that make your voice unmistakably yours.

single — Copy calling for just one voice actor. Also called "one-person copy."

"slate your name" — Before doing the take, record your name.

smile — As in "Remember to . . . ." And you'll warm up the copy, the casting director, the agent, the producer, the client, the engineer, yourself, and maybe a few others who have the good fortune to catch your smile.

soft-sell — See "passive commercial."

"spokes" — Short for spokesperson.

station I.D. — Very short spot in which the call letters of a particular radio or TV station are announced.

steps — Increasing the punch (energy) on each adjective when copy includes a long list of them.

step on lines — What happens when you overlap your partner's line by starting your own reading too soon.

storyboard — An artist's rendering of each camera setup.

studio — Room in which the talent actually records the copy. It's sometimes called the "announce booth."

tags — Short one- or two-line pieces of copy that either end a spot or stand alone to identify and describe the product.

take — The recording of a piece of copy. The first recording of that copy is referred to as "Take One"; subsequent recordings of that copy will be designated "Take Two," "Take Three" . . .

talk-back — The mic(s) over which the producer speaks to the talent in the studio. It's also used when the producer or engineer in the control room slates your name for you.

"talk to me" — Make your delivery more conversational.

tempo — How slowly or quickly you speak.

"throw it away" — Don't put any stress or emphasis on the reading. Make it light.

tone — Sound quality of the voice: harsh, sexy, nasal, etc.

under/over — As in "You were . . . ." Your delivery was either too short or too long, and didn't come in exactly on time.

"underscore it" — Highlight it.

units — Small voice-over market areas.

vocal characterization sheet — Developed by Pat Fraley. A form on which you can record helpful information about your individual characters.

voice-over hangover — The escalating doubts and fears that hit just after an audition. Take two positives and call your mom in the morning.

voiceprints — The vocal equivalent of fingerprints. Using samples of phonemes, experts can make positive identifications of speakers.

volume — How loudly something is said.

"warm up the copy" — Make your delivery friendlier or more intimate.

wild line — A line recorded during a pick-up session.

windscreen — A pop filter.

wind-sock — A foam device that fits over the mic to eliminate pops.

RESOURCES

The following lists of voice-over classes/workshops, graphic services, and agencies are included for your convenience only. We do not necessarily endorse them. This information is meant to be a random sampling; it is not comprehensive. If we have omitted a particular person who, or company which, provides any of the services mentioned, this should not be construed as a mark against them.

CLASSES

Austin/Dallas
Bob Michaels Studio
  bobsvoice.com   972-243-6086
VoiceWorks (Lainie Frasier)
  lfvoiceworks.com   512-441-6060

Chicago
Act One Studios
  actone.com   312-787-9384
The Audition Studio (Rachel Patterson)   312-527-4566

KRJ Productions/Audio One
beyondthewords.com   312-337-5111
Kate McClanaghan
voiceoverdemos.com   773-772-9539

Los Angeles

Cindy Akers
voicetraxwest.com   818-487-9001
Bob Bergen
bobbergen.com   818-999-3081
Wally Burr
blupka.com   818-509-1483
Louise Chamis   818-985-0130
Brian Cummings   323-497-8900
Delores Diehl's Voiceover Connection
voconnection.com   213-384-9251
Pat Fraley
patfraley.com   818-400-3733
Joanie Gerber   323-654-1159
Kalmenson & Kalmenson
kalmenson.com   818-342-6499
Carroll Day Kimble   323-851-9966
MJ Lallo
creatingvoices.com   818-980-6576
Ginny McSwain   818-548-7174
N.O.V.A. Productions   323-969-0949
Andrea Romano   818-997-8180
Susan Silo   818-725-3820
Cynthia Songé, Kooka Casting
blupka.com   818-763-8500
Sounds Great (A.D.R.) (Joan Ryan)   818-986-6062
Tobias Entertainment Group (Marice Tobias)
tobiasent.com   323-939-8679
Voices Voicecasting
voicesvoicecasting.com   818-980-8460
The Voicecaster
voicecaster.com   818-218-2342

VoiceWorksLA
  terryberlandcasting.com   310-571-4141
Nancy Wolfson
  braintracksaudio.com   310-472-4480

Minneapolis
Shirley Venard
  shirleyvenard.com   612-377-4868

New York
Drew Birns   212-580-4927
Joan Bogden (established only)
  vocoach@aol.com   212-534-1611
Karen Braga
  karen.braga@earthlink.net   212-928-4207
Madelyn Burns Casting   212-627-8880
Stuart Dillon
  adradtv.com   212-426-2466
Wendy Dillon   212-246-9611
Steve Harris' The Art of Voice
  theartofvoice@aol.com   212-517-8616
Glenn Holtzer   212-255-5112
Marla Kirban
  marlajkirban@hotmail.com   212-397-7969
Elisabeth Noone
  elisabethnoone.com   202-363-9493
VoiceWorks (Steve Garrin)
  vworks@aol.com   212-541-6592
Voiceovers Unlimited (Dan Duckworth)
  voiceoversunlimited.com   800-888-VEOH
David Zema (Voice of Success Program)
  davidzema.com   212-675-4978

Salt Lake City
Linda Bearman   435-645-8557
Christopher Miller
  chris@3graphics.com   801-548-3339

SCOTT SHURIAN
   voscott.com   801-359-1776

San Francisco

VOICE FACTORY
   thevoicefactory.com   415-776-8273

VOICE MEDIA (SUSAN MCCOLLOM)
   susanvoicemedia.com   415-956-3878

VOICE ONE (ELAINE CLARK)
   voiceoneonline.com   415-974-1103

VOICETRAX
   voiceover-training.com   415-331-8800

Seattle

I AM SOUND STUDIO
   iamsound.com   425-378-0223

KALLES-LEVINE CASTING   206-522-2660

VERONICA WEIKEL   206-547-3230

Toronto

ELLEN RAE HENNESSY   416-815-1318

SEARS AND SWITZER
   searsandswitzer.com   416-516-4612

VOICEWORX
   voiceworx.com   416-944-0440

Washington, D.C./Baltimore/Philadelphia/Virginia

ELISABETH NOONE
   elisabethnoone.com   202-363-9493

DEMOS

Austin/Dallas

DALLAS AUDIO POST (ROY MACHADO-SPANISH)
   dallasaudiopost.com   214-350-7678

SCOTCH PRODUCTIONS (GORDON NICOL)
   scotchproductions.com   214-559-4288

VOICEWORKS (LAINIE FRASIER)
lfvoiceworks.com — 512-441-6060

Chicago

BIG STRIKE PRODUCTIONS (RICHARD PICKREN) — 708-366-6040

BOSCO PRODUCTIONS
boscoproductions.com — 312-644-8300

CHICAGO RECORDING COMPANY (CHRIS SHEPARD)
chicagorecording.com — 312-822-9333

KRJ PRODUCTIONS/AUDIO ONE
beyondthewords.com
mindy@audioproducersgroup.com — 312-220-5423

Los Angeles

SUSAN BLU, BLUPKA PRODUCTIONS
blupka.com — 818-501-1258

WALLY BURR — 818-763-2618

LOUISE CHAMIS — 818-985-0130

CHUCK DURAN — 818-385-1000

CYNTHIA SONGÉ, KOOKA CASTING
blupka.com — 818-314-9434

DAVE & DAVE
everythingvo.com — 818-508-7578

MARC GRAUE — 818-953-8991

NICK OMANA — 323-969-0949

KRIS STEVENS ENTERPRISES — 818-225-7585

TOBIAS ENTERTAINMENT GROUP
tobiasent.com — 800-995-2096

VOICETRAX WEST — 818-487-9001

THE VOICECASTER
voicecaster.com — 818-218-2342

WORLD WIDE WADIO (JEFF HOWELL)
wadio.com — 323-957-3399

Minneapolis

BABBLE-ON RECORDING
babble-on-recording.com — 612-375-0533

COOKHOUSE RECORDING STUDIO
cookhouse.com   612-333-2067
VOICEWORKS RECORDING STUDIOS
mike@voiceworksrecording.com   612-338-8890

Nashville
SOUND RESOURCES (STEVE NABB)   423-499-8651

New York
STEVE HARRIS' THE ART OF VOICE
theartofvoice@aol.com   212-517-8616
GLENN HOLTZER   212-255-5112
ELISABETH NOONE
elisabethnoone.com   202-363-9493
ONE DESTINY PRODUCTIONS
1destinyproductions.com   212-629-6532
VOICEWORKS (STEVE GARRIN)
vworks@aol.com   212-541-6592
VOICEOVERS UNLIMITED (DAN DUCKWORTH)
voiceoversunlimited.com   800-888-VEOH

Salt Lake City
IF ENTERTAINMENT (JASON BARBER)   801-712-3404

San Francisco
VOICE ONE (ELAINE CLARK)
voiceoneonline.com   415-974-1103
VOICETRAX
voiceover-training.com 415-331-8200

Seattle
I AM SOUND STUDIO
iamsound.com   425-378-0223
STEVE MITCHELL PRODUCTIONS   206-547-3230

Toronto

CLARE BURT RECORDING STUDIOS
(JIM OR JOE DAVIDSON)   416-363-4421

Washington, D.C./Baltimore/Philadelphia/Virginia

LION & FOX RECORDING (ROB BURHMAN)
lionfox.com   703-941-6100
ELISABETH NOONE
elisabethnoone.com   202-363-9493
ROAR AUDIO & MUSIC
roaraudio.com   800-466-ROAR

DEMO DUPLICATION AND/ OR COVER GRAPHICS

Austin/Dallas

POINT 360
point360.com   214-744-0909

Chicago

BOSCO PRODUCTIONS   312-644-8300
CHICAGO RECORDING COMPANY (CHRIS SHEPARD)
chicagorecording.com   312-822-9333
KRJ PRODUCTIONS/AUDIO ONE
beyondthewords.com   312-337-5111
POINT 360
point360.com   312-280-8949
CREATIVEDIR.COM – CHICAGO RESOURCE GUIDE

Los Angeles

AT&T (MARK KNOOB)   323-466-9000
DYNAMITE DUBS   818-769-8800
POINT 360
point360.com   323-957-5500

| Rainbo Records | 310-829-0355 |
| Tape Specialty, Inc. (Stu Feldman) | 818-786-6111 |

New York

Angel Sound (Angel Sandoval)	212-765-7460
Point 360	
point360.com	212-627-2216
Steve Harris' The Art of Voice	
theartofvoice@aol.com	212-517-8616
Voiceovers Unlimited (Dan Duckworth)	
voiceoversunlimited.com	800-888-VEOH

San Francisco

Point 360	
point360.com	415-989-6245
Reeltime (Tony Johnson)	
reeltimedisc.com	415-459-7180

Washington, D.C./Virginia

| Lion Recording Services | |
| lionrecording.com | 703-569-3200 |

Anywhere

| Discmakers | |
| discmakers.com | 866-707-0012 |

AGENTS

Atlanta

Atlanta Models & Talent, Inc.	404-261-9627
Ted Borden & Associates	404 315-7343
People Store (Rebecca Shrager)	404-874-6448
Richard S. Hutchison Management	404-261-7824
VoiceCasting	877-449-1689

Austin/Dallas/Houston

ACCLAIM TALENT	512-416-9222
ACTORS ETC., INC.	713-785-4495
DB TALENT	512-292-1030
KIM DAWSON AGENCY	214-630-5161
MARY COLLINS AGENCY	214-871-8900
PASTORINI-BOSBY TALENT	713-266-4488
IVETT STONE AGENCY	972-392-4951
WILLIAMS TALENT	281-240-1080
SHERRY YOUNG/MAD HATTER, INC.	713-266-5800

Chicago

ENCORE TALENT AGENCY	773-638-7300
GEDDES AGENCY	312-787-8333
LINDA JACK TALENT	312-587-1155
LORI LINS LTD.	312-664-1107
NAKED VOICES (FORMERLY CED CHICAGO)	312-563-0136
SHIRLEY HAMILTON	312-787-4700
STEWART TALENT	312-943-3131

Detroit

THE I GROUP MODEL & TALENT MGMT.	248-552-8842
THE TALENT SHOP	248-644-4877

Los Angeles

ABRAMS ARTISTS AGENCY	310-859-1417
ACME/POSH VOICES	323-602-0370
ALVARADO REY	323-655-7978
ARTIST MANAGEMENT AGENCY	949-261-7557
MARIAN BERZON TALENT AGENCY	949-631-5936
BRAND MODEL & TALENT AGENCY	714-850-1158
BUCHWALD TALENT GROUP	323-852-9555
CASSELL-LEVY, INC.	323-461-3971
CUNNINGHAM, ESCOTT, DIPENE (CED)	310-475-2111
ENDEAVOR	310-246-3120

Hervey-Grimes Talent Agency	310-475-2010
Daniel Hoff Agency	323-962-6643
Imperium 7 Talent Agency (i7)	310-203-9009
Independent Artists Agency	310-550-5000
Innovative Artists	310-656-5172
International Creative Management (ICM)	310-550-4304
Kazarian/Spencer & Associates (KSA)	818-755-7570
William Morris Agency	310-859-4085
N2N Entertainment	310-247-2100
Osbrink Agency	818-760-2488
Sandie Schnarr Talent	310-360-7680
Solid Talent	323-978-0808
Special Artists Agency (SAA)	310-859-9688
Sutton, Barth & Vennari (SBV)	323-938-6000
TalentWorks Agency	818-972-4300
Arlene Thornton & Associates	818-760-6688
Tisherman Agency	323-850-6767
United Talent Agency (UTA)	310-273-6700
VOX, Inc.	323-655-8699
The Wallis Agency	818-953-4848

Minneapolis

Lipservice, Inc.	612-338-5477
Moore Creative Talent, Inc.	612-827-3823
Wehmann Models/Talent, Inc.	612-333-6393

Nashville

Chaparral Talent Agency (Kathy Carver)	423-238-9790
Talent & Model Land	615-321-5596

New York

Abrams Artists Agency	646-486-4600
Access Talent	212-331-9600
Ann Wright Representatives	212-764-6770
Arcieri & Associates	212-286-1700

ATLAS TALENT	212-730-4500
DON BUCHWALD & ASSOCIATES	212-867-1070
CUNNINGHAM, ESCOTT & DIPENE (CED)	212-477-1666
INTERNATIONAL CREATIVE MANAGEMENT (ICM/Celebrity)	212-556-5600
INGBER & ASSOCIATES	212-889-9450
INNOVATIVE ARTISTS	212-253-6900
PARADIGM	212-703-7540
WILLIAM MORRIS AGENCY	212-586-5100
FIFI OSCARD ASSOCIATES	212-764-1100

Salt Lake City

TALENT MANAGEMENT GROUP	801-263-6940

San Francisco

JE TALENT, LLC	415-395-9475
LOOK TALENT	415-781-2841
STARS, THE AGENCY	415-421-6272
TONRY TALENT	415-543-3797

Seattle

THE ACTORS GROUP	206-624-9465
TOPO SWOPE TALENT, LLC	206-443-2021

Tampa/Orlando/Miami

BERG TALENT & MODEL	813-877-5533
COCONUT GROVE TALENT	305-858-3002

Toronto/Montreal/Vancouver

AFLALO COMMUNICATIONS INC.	877-294-7272
ARTIST MANAGEMENT INC. (AMI)	416-363-7450
CHARACTERS TALENT AGENCY	416-964-8522
EDNA TALENT MANAGEMENT LTD	416-413-7800
FOUNTAINHEAD TALENT INC.	416-538-6888
FUSION ARTISTS INC.	416-408-3304
JAM TALENT MANAGEMENT INC.	416-362-2007

JORDAN & ASSOCIATES	416-515-2028
LeFEAVER TALENT MGMT. LTD	416-929-3112
LUCAS TALENT, INC.	604-685-0345
NOBLE CAPLAN ABRAMS AGENCY	416-920-5385
OSCARS ABRAMS ZIMEL & ASSOCIATES	416-860-1790
PACIFIC ARTISTS MANAGEMENT INC.	604-688-4077

Washington, D.C.

CENTRAL CASTING	202-547-6300